"The older I get, the hungrier I am to hear often hear it the clearest is through women stories. I can't sit close enough or long enou my faith feels fickle, I can lean in close and catch a whisper of God again through their words. Jennifer Camp has given us the gift of letting us pull up a chair in a circle of 40 women, where we can sit down and soak up their questions and God's answers. Wherever you feel dry or hurt or broken today, I am convinced this book has a message intended just for you."

—**Lisa-Jo Baker,** author of *Surprised by Motherhood* and community manager for (in)courage

"For every woman who questions whether her story matters, or who wonders what God thinks of all she brings before His feet, hope and healing are found in these pages. Jennifer Camp whispers truth from the heart of the Father to his daughters, awakening our remembrance of life breath that was first kissed at creation. This book will transform your days as it shows how to walk in the reality of a love that shapes our identity."

—**Kristen Kill,** author of *Finding Selah*

"Reading *Breathing Eden* was a sacred experience that moved me deeply, drawing me towards a very personal God who hears us, loves us, and never forsakes us. This book is for any woman whose life didn't turn out the way she planned—any woman who has doubted that God hears her cry. He hears. And He responds in a deeply personal way. Read this book and encounter the gentle whisper of God."

—**Jennifer Dukes Lee,** author of *The Happiness Dare*

"If you've ever felt lost, alone, afraid, mixed up, or beyond the place where you believe you can hear the voice of God, this book is for you. With relatable stories and tender words, Jennifer Camp has threaded this beautiful book through and through with the love of the Father for his beloved daughters. Settle into a cozy corner and open these pages to remind yourself that you were created to walk in the garden and hear the voice of God speaking over you. Turn these pages, oh Daughters of Eve, and remember what it feels like to breathe in Eden."

—**Logan Wolfram,** Speaker, and author of *Curious Faith: Rediscovering Hope in the God of Possibility*

Breathing Eden will delight your soul afresh as you unexpectedly uncover a way of communicating with God that is simple, organic, and life-changing.

—**Elisa Pulliam,** author of *Meet the New You*

breathing eden

CONVERSATIONS WITH GOD

ON LIGHT, FRESH AIR, AND NEW THINGS

jennifer j. camp

(z) | ZEALbooks

Published by Zeal Books
537 SE Ash St., Suite 203
Portland, OR 97214 USA
www.zealbooks.com

Cover Design: Connie Gabbert, Connie Gabbert Design + Illustration
Interior Design and typeset: Katherine Lloyd, The DESK
Interior Illustrations, Connie Gabbert, Connie Gabbert Design + Illustration
Author Photography: Nicole Moore, Storytree Studios

Library of Congress Cataloging-in-Publication Data

Names: Camp, Jennifer J., author
Title: Breathing eden: conversations with
god on light, fresh air, and new things / Jennifer J. Camp.
Description: Portland: Zeal Books, 2016 | includes index
Identifiers: LCCN 2016947123 | ISBN 9780997066944 (paperback)
ISBN 9780997066951 (ebook)
ISBN 9781613758724 (audio)
Subjects: LCHS: Christian life | Christian women–Religious life
Classification: LC Record available at http://lccn.loc.gov/2016947123

Printed in the United States of America

16 17 18 19 20 21 BP 6 5 4 3 2

to Abigail

and the daughters God loves

THE CONVERSATIONS

DEAR SISTERS,

When Brenda and I first heard Jennifer read from an early draft of *Breathing Eden*, we were sitting around our dinner table. From the first words, we knew we were hearing something special. Long after the guests had left that evening, we found ourselves talking about how powerful we felt the book would be for women who longed to hear God's perspective on the joys and struggles of their lives.

We all need that. We all need to hear His voice. We all need light, fresh air, and new things. So it's our great pleasure to offer this book to each of you, along with a prayer that God reveals his heart for you. For *you*.

May you see your life as He does, and may that be a breath of Eden.

Blessings to you,

Don (and Brenda) Jacobson

Ⓩ | **ZEAL**books

Arise . . . in the night . . . Pour out your heart
like water before the presence of the Lord!
Lamentations 2:19

For we know that the whole creation has been
groaning together in the pains of childbirth until now.
Romans 8:22

For the LORD *comforts Zion; he comforts all her*
waste places and makes her wilderness like Eden,
her desert like the garden of the LORD; *joy and gladness*
will be found in her, thanksgiving and the voice of song.
Isaiah 51:3

THIS BOOK BEGAN WITH AN EXPERIMENT. It began when a few questions arose during hours of conversation with friends and as many hundreds of emails went back and forth with readers of the popular *Loop* devotional, in which I wrote down what I sensed were God's whispers to his daughters, his girls.

Your stories, your questions, our discussions, prompted me to wonder: How are we changed when our hearts are open to hearing the voice of God? How can our conversations with him affect how we view ourselves, our lives, our pasts? How do our voices connect with the Voice who made us? And how can we hear God's voice, his truth, in the regular, ordinary moments of our lives?

What might God say to the woman whose marriage is ending or to the woman who has lost a child? How might God respond to the woman who is mad at him and wonders why he didn't rescue her when she was raped? What might he say to the woman overwhelmed with depression, or the woman struggling with her identity, or the woman who believes she needs to starve herself in order to get control of her life? Not all readers will connect with every story. And that's okay. It's God's voice we're listening for together.

The words of *Breathing Eden* are inspired by your stories. Not all the stories were communicated to me through conversations with you. Some were. But some were what I heard whispered to my heart. I pray you found yourself in these words. But mostly, I pray the whispers back to you, from God, as you write and speak out your own story, are the treasure.

So many of us find ourselves feeling lost in our own lives. It's so easy to lose perspective. To lose our way. To lose Jesus. To lose sight of him and thus to lose sight of ourselves.

We live in a demanding world that continually requires more and more from us. We get overwhelmed when we try to navigate our way through it on our own. But here's the brilliant news: We are not on our own! Every moment of our lives, every detail of our days are seen and known by the one who has won everything. God desires that we might come and draw more deeply into his heart. He whispers to us to come and know him as we are known. God does not wait to embrace us until we feel worthy of being embraced. He is captured by us now—in our imperfections, in our longings, in our glories, in our desperation, in our failings. The love of Jesus is not far away—it is close. He is close. And he desires for us to know him intimately, so that as we do, we come to face our days not with fear or a sense of being overwhelmed, but with strength and hope.

We can live lives of value and love. We can live lives that are free from shame, and are not bound by self-reproach or the accusations of the enemy and his lies.

The world needs you. Your world needs you. The people in your life whom you are called to love, serve, and walk alongside need you. But none of us can rise to the need or to the occasion of our lives without Jesus. And Jesus is here. He is Emmanuel. God with us. God is with us right now. He is our breath, our light, our hope, and our strength.

There is beauty and goodness in having knowledge about God. But knowledge alone will not see us through. We need to truly know God—to know that he is our champion. We need to grow in our ability to recognize his light, his breath, his call, his wooing, and his presence in our every moment. We need intimacy with God.

My friend Jennifer Camp is a woman who has an intimacy with Jesus that breathes life and light into her life. She is compelled by the love of God to invite other women into the deepest reality of this truth: that intimacy with Jesus is available to each one of us, and that truly knowing and experiencing his love changes everything.

So, dear ones, let light in. Let this tender and powerful book breathe life into you. Through the stories of these beautiful women, you will recognize your own story. You will be encouraged in your journey towards a deeper understanding of God's loving presence. He invites you to let that love inhabit your every moment. The words written here are designed to draw your heart more deeply into God's and to open your eyes to see yourself through his. You will be drawn into an intimacy with Jesus that is based solely upon his deep understanding and unconditional love for you. Oh, how we all need that. Oh, how I need that.

Jesus wants to share life with you. He wants you to embrace your story, and in doing so, come to know that God loves you intimately today, as you are. He sees you. He has not turned his face away. He wants to share your every moment.

Come, read, and accept Jennifer's invitation to breathe Eden.

Stasi Eldredge

JENNIFER

Introduction (the Desire to See)

Likewise the Spirit helps us in our weakness. For we do not know what to pray for as we ought, but the Spirit himself intercedes for us with groanings too deep for words.

Romans 8:26

I CAN'T BEAR IT.

That's what I tell God as my friend's words tumble out one after another. Her face is in her hands. She's perched on the edge of the chair, shoulders trembling, sobbing. No, my heart can't bear this. She definitely doesn't think she can.

I've been there. I know her desperation. I know weary, overwhelmed. I know what it's like—being convinced that hope is not for me. I am on my knees near her now, part of a circle, other sisters gathered around. Our hearts ache as we begin to pray—*No, don't remain here, dear one. You don't have to stay here. There is so much more than this moment—more above it, more below it. So much more beyond it.*

Our dear friend is in the place where walls press in and the

1

air lies thick and night feels all around. There is nowhere to go. Not when you've gotten to this place. Only shadows. No light. All around. She wants God but isn't sure how to reach him. *Are you here, God? Do you hear me, see me? Can you come?* She is confused. She wonders where God is. And we all wonder with her. All around. *Yes, I know this place.*

We gather close, these sisters and I, helping her forward, toward a different place. Toward new life. Toward the light that must be beyond here.

It's all about perspective, after all. God's perspective. She isn't trapped, no matter what she thinks now. I know the truth; I've escaped this place. I know now there is more to life than what we easily see.

What does it take to step into light when what surrounds us feels only dark? The sorrow feels too deep. The mistake seems too big. The wounds lie too buried. *Oh God, where is healing? Where is hope?* It is difficult to believe there is more than guilt, fear, worry, pain.

Pain can make us blind to—or desperate for—truth. Which is it going to be for her? For us? *Come on, girl. Come on.*

She sits there. We've held each other, shared a hundred cups of coffee, trusted each other with our stories. She is my sister, and she feels lost in this darkness. And because I love her, I feel stuck here, too. I want to carry her pain, to relieve it somehow. *How do we get to you, God? How do we stand and believe light can shine here, right here?*

I wonder.

I wonder—how does God see this? How does he see *us*? How does he see our stories, our pain, our struggles? How does he see the infidelity, the eating disorder, the abuse, the everyday anxiety that makes it difficult for us to lift our heads? How does he see our celebration, our worship, our experiences of freedom, hope, joy?

How would seeing God's view of our stories spur healing? Would it grant hope?

No matter our circumstances, we need God's perspective on them. We need to know how he sees us. *Come on, girl,* he says. *Let my light shine in.*

I am desperate for his eyes. I am desperate to see this pain and beauty—with new eyes. I am desperate to believe there is more than what my human frailty can see.

Do you want this too?

Prayer takes a listening, a looking deeper. Real prayer uncovers hope that is impossible to see on our own. God knows the wide-ranging emotions we feel—the cries of pain when we are overwhelmed and alone, the songs of joy when we are captured by his goodness and majesty. But what happens when he unearths the silent prayers we didn't know we had—of sadness or worship, confession, freedom?

How do our prayers sound to him? How does he see us, *really* see us, when we share our hearts with him? How does he respond? And how might this change us? I need to know.

This book consists of our prayers to God and his answers. Forty women. Forty prayers. Forty women's conversations with God.

But that's not all. Following each story is a personal invitation for you to enter into the dialogue with your own story. Forty invitations for your response. At the end of each conversation, you are invited to "Listen," to consider how you relate personally to what has been shared. You are invited to "Think," to wrestle with questions individually or in a group. You are invited to "Trust," to do something as a means of exploring what God might be communicating to you. And finally, you are invited to "Pray," to ask God to help you continue to process what he is doing in your heart.

My prayer is that in reading each of these conversations, and entering into them through prayerful response, you will recognize how light shines in your own life, even if you can see it only dimly (1 Corinthians 13:12).

Come listen to women who plead for God to be near. Come listen to women rejecting complacency. Come listen to women, choosing to seek God's freedom rather than fear in their everyday lives. Come listen to women who just want to speak to God and have him speak back. Come listen to women who just want to praise God and be heard. *Father, can I hear you? Will you heal me? How do you see things? Where were you in the night, when the darkness came and I felt abandoned and alone? You've come so many times; will you come again?*

You are in these pages. Your mothers and sisters and daughters and neighbors and girlfriends are, too. Your prayers are collected here, and heard.

Will you listen for God's response?

Do you want truth?

Do you want light, fresh air, and new things?

Turn the page.

In the Bright Place

WE KEEP THE WEDDING PHOTOS in an album tucked into the alcove underneath the stairs. It's next to the flower vases I almost never use, old mason jars and napkin rings stacked in the far corner. The album's pages are stiff, the cover's leather soft, worn from years of fingers. The kids pull it out sometimes, stretching it open across their little laps. *Mommy, sit with me. Tell me what the day was like, the day you and Daddy got married.*

I like to play the game with them, whispering the same stories over and over. My dress was my grandmother's, and my mom wore it too. Yes, I look like a princess. No, my shoes weren't slippers made of glass. Yes, Daddy looks so young. And yes, his smile is funny too.

I notice his hold of my hand, the two of us side-by-side down the red carpeted aisle. The girl in the photo is beaming. She believes there is only good ahead. I remember his first words to her, whispered in her ear after "I do." "You are my starlight. You are so beautiful."

That young girl, barely twenty-two, believed love would lead. She believed love would lead every future decision she would make. She believed the details would figure themselves out.

Was she just naïve?

Jesus, that girl didn't know what she didn't know. I think about her innocence; she believed she was going to be immune to tough times. Her story, of *course*, would be a happy one.

It never dawned on her she would face challenges in her marriage.

I wonder about her, this night twenty years later, easing my bare feet down the creaky stairs while the house sleeps. The old floorboards sigh, adjusting to changes in temperature, hot passes of day to the cool stretches of night.

Jesus, that girl of yours was bright and sweet but didn't know you like I know you now. Those dark moments I didn't see coming? That's how I found you. That's how I learned you stand steadfast. So many nights, knees tucked underneath my chin, bare feet on wooden floor. You taught me how to sit with you.

Can I just curl up next to you now? I lean against you. Will you hold me tight and let me stay here? I no longer have the answers that young girl had, yet I still want to believe I can make this marriage beautiful. I still want to believe I can live a story worth telling. I still want to believe I can paste pages of hope in an album my children will want to read. All because of you.

I am done chasing fairy tales. I am done faking this, done pretending everything is okay. I want your kind of real life. I want to choose love here—even if it is more work than I ever thought.

So give me wisdom, Jesus. Let me see the path. Set my feet upon it. Let me hear your voice: *This is the way. Walk in it.* I will receive your wisdom and stay here with you, your arms wrapped fast around me, never letting go.

I believe in you. I believe in light flooding dark places. I believe in change, hope, transformation.

I believe anything is possible with you.

MY DAUGHTER, I WILL STAY here with you. I will stay here as long as it takes. Holding you, drawing you close to me, is what I love to do most. I'm not going anywhere.

I love sitting here, too, you know. I love having you close. I will stay here with you. I will never leave you, if you want me to stay.

I love comforting you. I love reminding you how precious you are to me. I stay here with you, listening to the rise and fall of our chests. It's nice here, you know. You with me.

Real life here is better than anything you could dream up on your own. It is hard and beautiful, all in one. You weren't naïve when you believed love would lead. You did not have an incorrect view of marriage, only an incomplete one. The romance you yearn for is a true desire. It is good. I've placed within you the desire to be wanted, seen, pursued. It's how I've made you. The hard part is that love requires the dying to self.

Dying, you see, is never easy.

It is strange, I know, that love begins with death; but you know, as you look to my Son, that this is true.

Don't give up on romance. Don't give up on love leading. See that window there? It will not be night forever. See that hint of gold shining through? The sun can't help but come in. You know this: You can't close out light, child. You can ignore it. You can run. But it will shine all the same. You see it by knowing it's there, even if you only feel darkness around you.

The light is large enough to cover everything, each sliver of darkness that wants to remain. No darkness stays dark. No problem stays the same when the light touches it. Darkness cannot stand against the light. It has never overcome it.

I stay here with you, watching light come in. I stay here with you, helping you desire light. I stay here with you, teaching you what light feels like on the skin, on the face, how it reaches every dark place—each corner of this room, each corner of your heart.

Tell me where you want the light to shine. Ask me how you can open yourself up to it. Take my light in you and raise it high. In my name, nothing can withstand it.

I have given you the light, and I hold you in it, and you are filled with it, and you are not the same as you were before. All who see you and hear you and stay with you are responding to my light in you.

That light, daughter, lets nothing stay the same.

 **LISTEN**

Sit with Laine for a moment as she talks to God. What words resonate with you? What do you want to pray to God in response?

THINK

For at one time you were darkness, but now you are light in the Lord.
Walk as children of light. (Ephesians 5:8)

1. Laine says she didn't know God like she does now, after going through difficult times. Can you relate? What experience(s) in your life prompted you to deepen your relationship with God?

2. How do you crave wisdom? In what situation do you desire to see God's path for you?

3. How have you ever felt disillusioned? How do you crave God's light to shine on you? How do you desire his presence now?

 TRUST

Go outside in the sun or in a bright place near a window. Close your eyes. Lean back and feel the light on your face. Stay there for a few moments, eyes closed, shoulders relaxed. Let the light illuminate your face and touch your eyelids. Imagine God as light. Let the light cover you. Think about God's love blanketing you. Safe. Radiant. Warm. Beautiful.

 PRAY

Father, so many of your daughters are struggling. They want more of you and ache for your light to shine—in their marriages and in their hearts. I need you too, God. I can't figure out how to live well without your guidance. I don't have wisdom on my own. I can't fix all my mistakes. Help me trust and seek you with my whole heart. I believe your light floods the dark places of my heart and life. You bring hope, love, and joy. Flood my heart and life with your light. When I feel disillusioned, help me know your never-changing truth. Help me seek you and see you. I surrender all of me to your light. I am yours. In Jesus' name, Amen.

Then. Always. Now.

IT IS DEAFENING, this quiet.

Just Mark and me, together in a house that once shook with noise. Kids pounding through the narrow kitchen, footballs clench-ed under arms. Chairs scraping against wood floor so we can sit all together at dinner. Voices bickering about toothpaste mess on the counter and that too-small mirror in the hallway bathroom. I knew I'd miss it—tucking them in at night, giving backrubs under open windows in the summer dark, lives filling up these now near-empty rooms.

I knew how to be a mom. I knew how to sacrifice, stretched through the long days. But a wife? More than thirty years of love-filled chaos—five kids lived within these walls—and now silence. I'm not sure what to do now, how to remember how to connect with him. I search for signs, hints, any trace of a map showing how to be a loving wife, how to find my way back to Mark's heart.

There is hope for us, I think. In this new season, we sit on a new leather couch, side-by-side, no kids sprawled between us. He reclines to support his bad back. I sit next to him, needlework in my lap. We can watch whole television shows in the evenings, if we want. It's just us. We get to decide, together. It's nice.

But it's quiet.

We find each other's hand sometimes. We take walks in the orchard, the branches bent like lovers, praying as we walk the rows. How did we fall in love? Can I still remember? A mischievous grin, a saucy joke sparking his cheeks aflame, his jealousy for me, the sheets wrinkled up around our feet? Can I see him anew, now? How do I communicate my heart?

It seemed easier, I guess—the kids filling up the space between us all those years. Easier to stay busy with parenting. Easier to look past the man I had fallen in love with at only seventeen. Together and separate, during the years we forgot what energized *us*. We forgot what once made *us* crack up and smile. In the forgetting, we let ourselves forget who *we* were. Is it possible, Father, that we let ourselves forget the beauty of marriage, too?

My grandmother taught me love can't be corralled or tamed or controlled. "Love," she said, "is either going to take over every little space in the room or it's going to head right on out the door to find a home someplace else."

I've forgotten how to connect with Mark, God, but I won't give up. Will you give me hope? Will you make the love in our marriage fill the room, like my grandmother said? Can you make it fill a quiet house? Show me—what do I need to do? What do I say? How do I say it?

How do we find each other's heart again?

MY DAUGHTER, you feel like you are lost. But you are never lost if I know where you are.

Look—I am coming. Watch me lift the both of you. Watch me bend low and catch you up, just like your grandmother did when you were small. Watch—I do not hold back my love. Nor should you. I am yours. I am with you and I am not going anywhere.

You have a fierce strength—but now it is tender, wounded. It is difficult to recognize how your current relationships can be affected by the love—or lack of love—you experienced when you were little. You have been trying to convince yourself you are okay, and you are. But know the truth: You are only okay when you know that you are loved.

Do you know how much I love you, right now, just as you are, my darling? Do you know I have always loved you more than you could imagine?

Your struggle is not what you think it is.

You see the symptom. I shall cure the disease.

You pray for a flower. I must nourish the root.

You want to reconnect with Mark? You want to love him with freedom and abandon? You want me to teach you how to love? You must do something first. Return now to the place where *we* began. Remember when you first knew me. Remember when you believed I was close. Next, let me show you where I was in the hard moments. I have always been near.

Because in the moments when you felt abandoned, ignored, unimportant—I was with you, my daughter.

Because in the moments when you ached for the "I love you" that never came—I was with you, my daughter.

Because in the moments after you were married, when you tucked the children in and you slept by yourself, so many nights, I was with you, my daughter.

You grew up thinking you were too much to love. Too needy. Too loud. Too present. Too weak. And you've carried these lies into your marriage. It is time to hear this, my darling. I want you to know this and live like you believe it: You were never too much. You were never too much to spend time with, have fun with, dance with, laugh with, hold hands with. You are beautiful and you are cherished.

This is what I want you to remember:
You are the one I choose.
You are the one I've always wanted.
You are the one I want to be with.
Then. Always. Now.

 LISTEN

Phoebe is in a new season. Her children have moved out and she tries to reconnect with her husband. Not being shown love when she was young makes it more difficult for her to trust that she has what it takes to love her husband well. She asks God for hope. Was God's response what you expected? What do you want to say to God in response? Write your prayer to him.

THINK

Beloved, let us love one another, for love is from God, and whoever loves has been born of God and knows God. (1 John 4:7)

1. What is the biggest life change you've experienced? How did that transition affect your most important relationships?

2. What relationship presents the biggest challenge to you right now? How do you struggle to love that person?

3. God's response to Phoebe includes insight into her previous relationships as a child, and how they affect how she loves people now. How do you relate to what God says to Phoebe?

 TRUST

Sit down. Think of yourself at eight years old. Remember what you looked like, what you liked to do. Now consider: Were you loved? Did you feel cared for and adored by the people in your life? With God's help—listening for his voice—write a letter to your eight-year-old self, telling her what is true about her, the things God thinks about her. Then write a letter to God, asking him to help you love a person in your life right now with whom you are having trouble.

PRAY

Father, I don't always know how I need you. While I ask for help with one thing, you point me toward a different struggle—the root of my pain. You invite me into deeper healing. Please help me surrender and accept your love and help. Reveal to me what prevents me from loving others with a full heart. Help me surrender those obstacles to you. Remove them from me. Help me go forward, in freedom, loving others the way you love. In Jesus' name, Amen.

Prayer Circles and Wringing Hands

GOD, LET'S DO THIS QUICKLY. You know I'm uncomfortable praying. I struggle to find the right words when I'm talking to you. I second-guess each word I say. I hear how you're safe. I read how you love me just as I am. But I can't help comparing myself to my friends as they pray aloud.

I feel like a child stumbling over my words, nervous that my simple prayers don't convey enough depth, at least not the depth of love my friends seem to feel toward you. Oh, they share such beautiful prayers aloud to you! Do you know I love you, too? Are my simple prayers, the ones in my head, getting through?

The thing is, you made me a leader in many ways. I can stand up and address a room full of people. I can lead complicated projects and manage details and organize large groups. I am decisive and able to handle stress in chaos. But when it comes to sitting down and *praying*, either alone or in a group of friends who love me and know me? My heart races. I want to run out of the room.

If you are safe, why do I struggle to talk to you? I have trouble believing there is not a certain right way to pray. Could it be true that some people can hear you better than I can? The women in my Bible study group talk to you like you are right there, in the room, listening. They act like they can tell you anything. They confess their fears, their regrets, their desperate need for your peace and joy and help. But me? I guess I struggle, still, with thinking of you as a person, as a friend.

It is confusing, really, to think about how you know all about me, and yet you invite me to talk to you. It seems that you want a relationship where words convey more than words, a connection of heart and mind between God and daughter, father and child. I fear I don't know how to find the perfect words. I fear I can't hold up my side of the bargain.

I want to learn how to relate to you like the women in my prayer group do. I am envious of their relationships with you. I want that kind of relationship too, I think. I know you say it is good to have the faith of a child, but I am not childlike in my faith; rather, I am childlike in my lack of confidence. I fear I don't have what it takes to connect with you.

I feel pretty alone here, even in this group of friends. Can you hear my heart speak these words to you now? I can't say this out loud, but . . .

I don't know what I'm doing.

YOU DID IT just now, you know. You prayed. Praying is talking to me. And this? What we're doing here? This is a relationship blooming—because this here is a conversation. You don't need to worry about what to say to me or how to say it. You don't need to worry about fitting in or measuring up in any prayer group or women's Bible study.

You don't know what you're doing, but I do, and I love it. Keep it up.

You don't need to think about what it's supposed to look like to love me. How the world sees is not how I see. And what I see is a bold and tender warrior woman who loves and does not hesitate to do the hard thing when it counts.

Don't doubt how I've made you. But look to what I'm doing in you.

Isn't prayer about communicating your heart to me? And in prayer, your heart aligned with mine, you worship. Prayer is not about words, anyway. It is conversing with me with more than speech—your mind turned to me as you prepare your presentation at work; your listening for me as you serve, expecting me as you rest, looking for me as you walk, finding me as you dream. I love the different ways I have made my daughters and sons to speak to me—with their hearts, their hands, their mouths, their souls and spirits united with me. I give you your own language, not just in words, to speak to me. Be bold, daughter. Claim how I've made you to pray. I have more to show you. I have more of my presence to give you. I want you to claim it. I want you to know it.

Come on now, girl. The two of us together?

We've got this.

 **LISTEN**

Claire doubts her ability to connect with God. Can you relate to her? How do you feel about God's response? Write a prayer telling God about it.

THINK

Then you will call upon me and come and pray to me,
and I will hear you . . . (Jeremiah 29:12)

1. What is your biggest obstacle in praying to God? What are obstacles you face in hearing him speak?

2. How does fear of what others think ever get in the way of you praying aloud to God?

3. What does God say to Claire that you find personally encouraging?

4. Do you relate more to Claire, or to the other women in her group who pray easily?

 TRUST

Think of an activity you love to do, an activity that allows you some space to be by yourself with God. It could be listening to music, taking a walk, baking a cake, painting a canvas, anything that brings you joy. Set out to do that activity, and invite the Holy Spirit to do it with you. Ask God to help you be present with him while you do this activity with him. Watch for him. Listen for him. Let this be your prayer.

PRAY

Father, you have made me perfectly, and I am designed to communicate with you. Teach me more of who you are and the language you have given me to speak to you. I want to know our language, the way you have made me to engage with you and know you. I surrender to you my fear of what others think. Let me talk to you freely, knowing that when I am in your presence I am safe. I trust your words are in my heart, and you are in me. In Jesus' name, Amen.

Camouflage

THE PAVEMENT BLAZES UNDER MY FEET, my thin ballet flats not the best choice for the park. But they're leopard-print, and they're *cute*. Squished, hot toes are a small sacrifice to camouflage how I feel. Discouraged. Tired.

I cut my long hair last week. It's a bob now. Jonathan pulls on everything, his chubby hands soft and strong. It's unfamiliar, falling in my eyes. I push it back, the sun hot on my face.

I pull the stroller shade down so the sun doesn't hit the little guy. We're walking to the park, then to preschool to pick up big brother Lucas. Jonathan can't do much more than tumble around the sandbox or sit in the baby swing. He doesn't care whether we're here or in our big backyard. But I need to get out. That house gets oppressive. Chores never end. Doing laundry, folding diapers, picking up toys, making food I scarcely taste.

I wanted to be a mom. I wanted to stay home with these precious kids. I quit my job, surrendered my identity—the young, just-out-of-business-school-turned-professional. I believed my choice was narrow, just one or the other—be a mom or work. (Are these my only choices, God?) I didn't want to miss puddle-jumping, block-building, hand-holding, park-playing days like this one. I am grateful to have had the opportunity to make that decision. I am. I just didn't know I would struggle so much. I didn't know this would be so hard.

For now, the baby sleeps. And I walk—my flats and short hair a silly attempt to feel normal. I want to look cute for the moms at the park and at preschool pick-up. I want to look like I know what I'm doing. Not lost. Not lonely. Not sad.

I thought I would feel different, God. I thought I would do this better—that I would be more organized and wouldn't feel so depleted all the time. I said I wanted to stay home with my babies, and I know it is so amazing that I can. But here is what is hard to admit, even to you: I don't like it as much as I thought I would. I'm afraid I'm not good at it. I'm even less confident now that we have two.

I'm going to mess them up, God. I *know* I am. I lose my temper; I raise my voice. And when I am not yelling out loud, I feel like I am screaming inside. I know that's an exaggeration. That sounds so melodramatic, "screaming inside." But no other words feel right.

Why do I feel so trapped, so stuck? I don't know who I am, or what I love to do, or what it is that might be fun for *me* anymore. I should feel parenting is so fun, so completely fulfilling. I'm sorry that, right now, I don't, and it isn't. I'm sorry for who I am. I'm sorry I am so far from you and don't know how to find my way back.

Can you help me find my way back?

We're at the park now. I'm going to take off these hot shoes and wake Jonathan and sit in the sandbox with him in the shade. It's cool here; I can feel myself quiet. A few moms are at the swings with their babies. I hear the children laughing. My Jonathan is giggling now, too. So, I'll take a deep breath.

A deep breath.

THE SHOES LOOK GOOD. Really. The hair, too. You're beautiful.

It's nice here, just sitting with you. Your Jonathan is precious. The way you mother him is precious, too.

You can be angry. I can take it. You can be sad. I can take that, too. Keep running to me when you are sad and overwhelmed, and I will give you what you need to get through a day. You think you are camouflaged, but I see all.

You can do this, you know. You can mother him and love him, and I will help you find your way. You ask me what you love? Who you are?

Let me tell you what I see: I see *you*. I see you in the early mornings when the baby is crying and you rise. I see you bend to scoop him up out of his crib, hear how you sing to him. I watch how you stumble, *so* tired, back to a rumpled bed.

May I sing to you now? May I sing to you, my daughter who is found?

Lift up your head, my darling. Lift up your head and see me looking at you. I have made you with beauty. I have made you with strength. I have made you with tenderness, a soft heart for me that will sustain you. I sustain you. Keep your heart soft, and I will sustain you. Keep yourself vulnerable, and I will lift you. Keep yourself close to me, and I will show you, step-by-step, what you love, what I see in you.

There's a lot coming, dear one. You are both a light that shines and a warrior in my name. How this looks—your life in me—will unfold as you trust me. I keep creating in you, dear one. I love being with you as we partner in your work, bringing what is to come.

Yes, I see you. And I want you to begin this day again, knowing I see you, knowing I know you. I dance over you. My gladness overflows.

You are my dear heart, my bright flower. I father you and I mother you. I care for you and you rise again, letting me lead, letting me take charge, letting me be the door you walk through each day when you are lost and you are wondering how, again, you can face another day.

You don't need to face another day alone. You can greet each day with me. You can rise with me, stay with me, listen for me. In the creak of the highchair at lunchtime. In the jingling of toys as Jonathan and Lucas laugh and cry and play. In the hush or whimpers of the night.

My strength is enough for you. My presence is with you. My Spirit is in you.

I sustain you, never leave you. There is good coming.

There is good right here.

 **LISTEN**

Lucy asks God to help her surrender who she is and who she believes she is supposed to be. How have you struggled with your identity? Write down your prayer to God in response.

_____

_____

_____

_____

_____

_____

_____

_____

_____

_____

_____

_____

_____

_____

_____

_____

_____

_____

_____

_____

THINK

Call to me and I will answer you, and will tell you great
and hidden things that you have not known. (Jeremiah 33:3)

1. When have your expectations not measured up to reality? What emotions did you feel? How have you coped with disappointment in these situations?

2. When do you most often disguise how you really feel? What do you use as camouflage? Clothes? Words? Actions?

3. How does knowing that God is present with us in all things, despite our expectations or our disappointments, affect how you view your situation, this moment, right now?

4. How does it feel to know God sees you in your fullness, knows the truth of who you are—so beautiful, so glorious, so perfectly made by him?

 TRUST

Choose a favorite love song or poem or piece of music that brings you joy and helps you feel close to God. Listen to it as if God is singing the words or playing the music to you. Stay here, with Jesus, listening to the music; be attentive to your emotions. Tell God which lines in the song are your favorite, which ones you want to keep close.

PRAY

Father, you are unashamed of me; your love is wild and perfect. I love how you have made me. I love how I don't have to hide from you, no matter what I am feeling. You give me a voice to call out to you, and you answer. You reveal yourself to me, showing how you are present with me, how you care for me, how you hold me and never let me go. I have what it takes to love those you've given me to love. I have what it takes to get through this day, holding your hand. Help me do all these things, knowing I stay with you. In your name, Jesus, Amen.

How the Warm Water Splashed

THESE PEWS ARE AS HARD AS EVER, the pine polished and smooth. It's been a while since I've been here. But I could have drawn it all for you. It's so familiar. The crimson carpet in the middle is more worn, for sure, the edges frayed and soft. Two decades ago I stood at the pulpit of this old country church, my teenage self thinking I had a lot to say about a God I thought I knew.

It was our high school baccalaureate. I stood up there in this little church catty-corner to the school and told my friends in the pews all the things my Sunday school teachers had told me were true: "God, you are big and you are faithful and you have our futures all figured out for us, even if we don't know yet what they are!"

I believed a lot of it, I guess. I believed you were here. I believed you were in charge and had a halfway-decent plan.

But you know, God? That seventeen-year-old didn't have a clue.

God, what did I have to say about you then, really? Cute ideas,

29

not convictions. You were aloof and intimidating, a God to believe in so I could get to heaven, a God to talk at so everyone would know I believed in Jesus. Hell sounded horrible, with all that fire and gnashing of teeth.

I didn't know, then, that anywhere I am without you is hell.

I put myself into a slow, smiling hell I created, crowding you out with my selfishness, believing you loved me, but not appreciating it. I took you for granted.

It's hard to admit it, but you know it all already. I might as well say it. I was so used to having parents who gave so much for me, so sacrificially and lovingly, I was comfortable with the idea of a God who sacrificed himself for me. A good girl like me *almost* deserved it, after all! That's how full of myself I was. I was comfortable with your love, your sacrifice. It didn't seem crazy, then, that you died for me. It didn't seem like much at all. I really thought I was worth it.

Oh, gosh, I'm sorry. I'm so sorry.

I was proud. I worked so hard pretending I had it all together. What counted was that I was a nice girl, a responsible girl who'd been baptized with the other kids in Sunday school and sat with her parents each week in the stiff-backed pews.

But you know the real story.

You know I lied to my parents and my friends. You know I killed a baby in my womb a year before. I didn't want anyone to know I wasn't the good girl they all believed I was. They *couldn't*. They *couldn't* know. I wanted to be that fake good girl so badly. At least I think I did, even when I knew she was a lie.

Do you remember when I was baptized? Of course you do. This church, Palm Sunday. I was eleven. That was a good day. I stood in that cotton sheet-like robe over my T-shirt and shorts, in a tub cut out of the floor, right under where the altar usually stood. My bare feet planted on rough green and blue checked carpet as I waited my turn to step into the water. It was warm when I did, and I stepped down to Pastor Ben, who wore a white T-shirt and not his usual suit and tie. His eyes were kind and he held my hand. He asked me if I believed in Jesus, and if I believed Jesus loved me, and if I loved him, and if I wanted to be baptized. And I said yes.

I remember that girl in the water. I remember her face. I remember she held onto Pastor Ben's strong forearm so much like her dad's. He put a white handkerchief in one hand, and then, with the other, he supported her back. He tipped her backward, and warm water splashed over her whole body, her whole heart and head. And then he pulled her back on up. She believed she was different then, somehow. And when she stepped into that rainbow-striped seersucker dress her mom had made her, she believed she was transformed. She was beautiful, and when she turned, her arms out wide, the circle skirt lifted a bit as she twirled.

God, where did she go? Where is that girl in the water? I can't find her.

She's still lost.

I REMEMBER THE GIRL in the water.

Do you know that I held you before you were born? My arms wrapped tight around you, my care for you perfect in your innocence.

You know the story now: You struggle to hear me when you don't believe I am good. You struggle to receive me when you don't believe I am near. You are the daughter I held, and I hold still. I have never left you. I have always loved you. No matter what you've thought. No matter what you've said. No matter what you've done.

You don't need to guard your thoughts from me. You don't need to hide, or try to fix yourself up. Even in your weakness you are beautiful to me. In the places you are most afraid, I want to restore you—show you the truth in you I've always seen.

You are not a disappointment, darling one. I have never turned away from you. I've always whispered to your heart. But it is now, in the laying down of who you were, that I speak.

It's time to drop the lies now. Time to lay down the regrets. It's time to let light shine in. I overcome all darkness. I will overwhelm you, restore you to what has always been my plan: beauty, delight. You will be a daughter free and powerful. Unafraid.

I have been with you in all moments, in all pain. My love for you has never wavered. You have fought a foolish fight, lived life as if it were a contest.

That is over.

Rest now in my arms. I am here. I hold you.

And you should know—I hold your child here, too.

 **LISTEN**

Cara is filled with guilt and shame as she remembers her past. After hearing Cara's conversation with God, what is your prayer? What do you want to say to God in response?

THINK

*If we confess our sins, he is faithful and just to forgive us our sins
and to cleanse us from all unrighteousness. (1 John 1:9)*

1. Does any part of Cara's story resonate with you? What part?

2. Have you ever believed God's love for you is dependent upon your behavior?

3. Have you ever doubted God's presence with you, or his desire to speak to you?

4. What past sin or present regret do you think he is hoping you confess to him now? In his response to Cara, what did you most need to hear God say?

 TRUST

How we think God sees us shapes how we see him. What words come to your mind when you think of God? Based upon your unique experience with him, write down in a journal a list of words that describe his qualities, his personality, even how you imagine his appearance to be. (Don't worry about what is "correct"; don't try to guess the right answers from Scripture.) No censoring. No holding back. When you're done, read it over and jot down personal experiences—a few words is fine—that explain the reasoning behind each word you chose to describe God.

Next take a deep breath—maybe even a walk—to clear your head. Then take another look at what you wrote down and read each word back to God. Talk to him about what you think of him. Share with him each experience that explains, in your opinion, why you feel the way you do.

Now surrender each one of those words to him. Ask him to show you what is true and what is false about what you wrote. Look at your list again and be aware of which words feel a little "off" and which words feel true, even if you aren't yet sure why. If you can, share your list with friends who love you and who love God. Have them do the activity, too, and then listen to God's heart together. Ask the Holy Spirit to point you to Scripture that reveals the truth of God's character. Ask the Holy Spirit to help you rewrite your list: Get out a blank piece of paper. Listen and write. Be patient. This might take a while—or it might take only a few minutes. Wait on him. Listen.

 PRAY

Father, I confess I have not known you. I confess I have not feared you. I confess my pride—I have cared more about what other people think of me than about living the truth of who I am in your love. I surrender my heart and my mind to you, with my present, my future, and my past. I believe you come and redeem all things. I believe you redeem me. In Jesus' name, Amen.

It's time to drop the lies now, darling.
It's time to lay down the regrets.
It's time to let light shine in.
I overcome all darkness, my love.

When the Blue Jay Sings

IT WAS A DAY SO MUCH like this one, the day we saw the backyard of our first home. There was a blue jay perched high on the wood fence, right where the property slopes to the creek. He sat there proud and stubborn, letting us know *he* was the boss of *this* garden. I let him know pretty soon, in the weeks after we moved in, that he was going to have to make room for me out there, too.

We chose this house together, a few years after getting married. We had been living in a condo in the city after we graduated from business school, and this was the house I had dreamed I would live in someday—with my husband and my kids and maybe even a dog to run and play in the yard.

The house was wide, the width of the property, with picture windows and a redwood deck that faced the backyard and looked out onto the trees. The tall trees, with their elegant branches and tinkling leaves, looked like aspens to me. Dan said there are no aspens in California, but that is something I never wanted to believe. (And I'm pretty sure he's wrong.)

Whatever they are, the trees in the backyard are beautiful. Their leaves sparkle like jewels after it rains. At the end of storms, raindrops linger, like they were the grand finale of some fancy party anyone was invited to attend. I liked looking out the back windows and walking out into the fresh air, touching damp leaf edges with my fingers. Me, in my jeans with the ripped-up knees. No dog, just the old blue jay, watching me and scratching for worms in the far corner of the backyard.

The air is fresh this evening. Cool. It is the evening light I love best, the way it paints shadows on the grass, sunlight saying good-night to the trees. I like it here, and I wish Dan were here, too. The kids miss him; my little Nick cried himself to sleep again, his eight-year-old eyes still puffy and red as he climbed up the school bus steps to go to school. Dan's been gone a few months now.

I can feel it still, the tearing of this one flesh. I don't know how to be whole again. It's hard to believe in goodness for this family now, now that we've torn it apart. It's hard to love anything or anyone beyond these kids.

This house? I thought we would be together here forever. He would bring wine out to the deck, two glasses tucked in one hand. I'd light a candle and we'd talk, catching up with one another after being apart during the day. Sometimes we wouldn't talk at all, and that was okay, too. He was my best friend. I can hardly believe I can't make this all okay.

This isn't the dream I dreamed, for my children or for me. I want a new ending. I don't like this one—me, in the shadows, in the backyard, with that old stubborn jay.

God, where were you?

Where are you now?

I can't keep pretending to smile.

I KNOW YOU THINK I didn't hear the prayers. I know you think your cries for help went unheard. I know, in the darkness, when you went under the night sky and cried to me, you felt angry and alone. You wanted to yell at me. Where was I? Where could I be found?

Always here. I have never left your side.

I see that day when you first saw this home. It is then for you, it is now for me. You notice the blue jay, hear the creaking trees as they sway in the breeze. You glimpse the light shining bright through not-yet-opened windows. You grab Dan's hand and he holds you. It is a beginning.

My darling. I am here. I am always.

I am sorry this family was torn in two. I am sorry your heart feels split into pieces. I am sorry you think you are not able to love anyone, ever again.

Now is tomorrow's then. Tomorrow is now to me. Trust me—you are more than what you can see; you are light shining bright, my love. You are my daughter in rays of sunshine, even when skies are dark all around and the storm's rains are pouring fast. You do not have to be strong.

Come to me now. Your children will see you coming to me, and then they will see me. Cling to me, and your home will be a sanctuary, my place where I am with you, beyond these walls, beyond the beauty of this yard. I welcome you home, to a new place, and I repair the broken parts of your heart, and I make them whole again.

There is more for you, child. Come and be, in a quiet place with me. Let me be the one who whispers to your heart. Let me be the one who builds you a new home with me. What is ahead will be good. You will know it. You will enter in.

 LISTEN

Janie is reeling, wounded from the loss of a marriage, a dream. How do you respond to her conversation with God? What is your prayer in response?

THINK

And we know that for those who love God all things
work together for good, for those who are called according
to his purpose. (Romans 8:28)

1. How have you struggled with accepting a new ending, a dream or expectation that didn't turn out as planned?

2. Do you believe God never leaves you, that he is present with you in all moments?

3. What do you imagine it means to make God your home?

 TRUST

Find a pen and a journal. Then get comfortable and take a few deep breaths. Without writing anything yet, think about what image(s) occurs to you when you complete the following sentence: "I will be happy when . . . " Spend a few minutes with those images. Write them down.

Next, finish this sentence: "I was so happy that moment when . . . " Reflect on what brought you happiness. What was it like? What were you doing? Think about that moment for a few minutes, then describe it in writing.

Look at what you wrote. Look how the two images are different from one another. Is your dream of imagined future happiness different from the actual moments of happiness you have experienced? Ask God to show you what he wants you to see—what wisdom he wants to give you.

PRAY

Father, I give you my dreams, the ones I've held close, the ones that haven't turned out like I had planned, the ones shattered. Help me heal. I give you my expectations, for me and for my family. I pray for restoration of what has broken, for what has torn. I want to believe there is nothing you can't make whole. I do believe. In Jesus' name, Amen.

Maps, Dust, and Blood

THE SUITCASE LIES OPEN ON the bedroom floor next to heaps of laundry the kids piled while I was gone. Scent of the trip lingers, infused in more than just the cotton fabric of my clothes. I run my fingers over the suitcase's nylon threads, the suitcase that rolled from my house and through the airport and into the soft foreign dirt I call my second home. I almost feel the dirt on my skin—with the memory of cheek against cheek, of crinkles around children's eyes when they smile.

Before my first trip to Africa, I didn't know what it meant for a heart to split right open. Do you remember the day I walked into the village for the first time? We bumped along for hours in the van. When we turned onto the village road, the children came from behind the trees, ten or more carrying bundled babies on their little backs. I didn't know children so young could carry infants and run and smile.

They invited us in, our whole team. They welcomed us into their homes with thatched straw roofs and dirt floors. We stood in single rooms, mud dividers separating the adults' beds from where the older children kept warm at night with the goats. I couldn't communicate with the women like I wanted to. I didn't know their language, and they didn't know mine. But the children did, since they had been learning it in school. So we were still able to have conversations, stilted and awkward, but so *good*.

While I longed to go, I didn't know how I could be useful. I was a teacher with a heart for connecting with people, but what real help is that? I couldn't speak the language. I was in a new-to-me culture, one I didn't yet understand.

But this is what you taught me—what you showed me about love and family and the truth of brothers and sisters around the world. Language? Knowledge? They are both overrated. The foundation to relationship is trust, understanding. Love.

We didn't need words to connect. We read each other's faces. We used gestures. I showed photographs from home. It was by looking at each other's eyes, though, that we could understand and trust the most. I returned. Then went back. And again. And again . . . and . . .

I see you in Africa, so far from my American home. After each trip, I understand a bit more how you remain, God—you are everywhere I can't see. You teach me there is no difference between a family of blood and family on the other side of the earth. We share your blood, Jesus. We are one because it is your blood we share.

I am with you, my God. You lead. I follow. It's okay that I don't have the map, the next steps, the reason why you nudge me to see the world through your eyes and not my own. For it is my second home now. I have gone six times. I'm learning the language and developing relationships with this second family of mine. Sometimes I think about how I never would have met them if I hadn't packed that first bag and left what was comfortable, predictable, and known. In going, I get a better glimpse of how you see.

I want more of that, Father. I want to take risks and do what doesn't feel safe. I want you to connect us with your love. I don't need to know why you nudge me forward before I respond. I trust you, then step. I don't want to miss being with you. I don't want to miss discovering more of who I am. I don't want to miss learning more of all the love that you have.

So, yes. Yes, I will continue to go with you, your daughter, your fearless one.

WHAT NOW, MAY I say? You think you are going to them. They think they are welcoming you. I am ever with you all.

Go forward. The road is clear.

I am your map.

I am your guide.

I am there already, and will be here when you return. Forever.

 LISTEN

Kelsie realizes how God connects his children through his love, despite differences in geography, wealth, and beliefs. How do you describe Kelsie's relationship with God? What prayer do you want to write to God in response?

THINK

> *He said, "Come." So Peter got out of the boat and*
> *walked on the water and came to Jesus. (Matthew 14:29)*

1. When have you pursued a relationship with someone with whom it seemed you had nothing in common? What happened? How did you feel?

2. Where are you willing to follow God? What makes you open to following him?

3. Where do you think God is leading you now?

 TRUST

If you can, stand up and go outside. If you can't, imagine going down the street in your neighborhood. Look around. Turn right or turn left. Find someone you have trouble connecting with, maybe someone with whom you've never spoken. As you walk, pray over each home you walk by, blessing the home with God's provision and peace and goodness. Ask God to help you love these neighbors. Be expectant for the Holy Spirit to whisper to your heart; look for the opportunities God brings for connection.

PRAY

Father, no matter where I go, you are with me. I want to go where you lead. Let me be your fearless one, your faithful one. Help me recognize today where you are—for you are in all things; you are in all places. Fill and equip me. Help me seek your heart and follow you without hesitation. There is no other way I want to live. In your Son's precious name, Amen.

The middle place

IT'S COLD TODAY, THE SKY white-blue. I pull my sweater over my shoulders and hug my elbows to my chest. Bare feet, toes squishing through wet sand. I feel hollow inside, heavy. The fog crawls gray and slow. I could walk this beach until the sun shines bright and not feel its rays warm my skin. I want to be cold, I think—frozen, unmoved.

I touch the thigh where I inject the medicine twice a day. *Let it work.* Why, God, would you give me this desire to have a child, when it remains, year after year, unfulfilled?

I am waiting. Months of mornings walking this beach, the ache for a child so heavy I feel I will surely drown. Am I greedy? Is it okay for me to feel discontent?

I struggle to surrender my desire for more. What about the dream you gave me, God? The cry from a crib in the morning, the smell of sweet skin, a life to hold and shield and love with my whole heart?

You know I would love this baby, right? You know I would give everything to love him or her the way you love me? You know I would not take being a mom for granted, and I would do my best to surrender my life to you?

Oh, Father, may I ask again? May I be the daughter who believes you give good gifts? May I accept your gift of faith? Is it possible I ask for too much?

I am going to sit here now, stay on this sand and watch these waves crash hard on shore. I'm going to keep asking you questions; I'm going to keep pursuing you. I want to believe that it's all going to be okay—even right now, when this feels so hard.

I COULD walk this beach with you forever, Hannah. Did you see those gulls swoop down over there? They are looking for fish. I love watching them, how they glide, wings spread, so beautiful. And then they dive, so unexpectedly. I love how they fly with confidence, intent on the hunt, knowing what they need to do and where they need to go. The wind lifts them, they glide; they swoop again, searching the waters. The waves promise sustenance. They return to what provides.

My daughter, you can hold my hand or you can let go. I will be here all the same. But at this moment, look around. Enjoy this place, right now. In the midst of the wondering, the searching, the questions—hunt the beauty of here, even in the midst of pain. There are good things hidden in the waters.

You ask me—can there be beauty in pain? Can there be hope in suffering?

You wonder—can there be joy in the hard places, where there is no clear answer?

Look to me. Look where I am, in the midst of the hard things. Look to me—I am here, present with you. Look to me—plunge for the truth placed already in your heart. I am with you even when you can't see me. I am with you even when questions aren't answered. I am with you, present, when all feels only night.

Every question will be answered soon. But I change every question.

This beach will be where we stay, even in your yearning. My presence will bring contentment, if you let it. My presence will bring hope, if you want it. My presence will bring joy, if you seek it.

I am your guide, your landing place—and I will teach you, soon, to fly.

 **LISTEN**

Hannah, struggling with infertility, is in a place of yearning and uncertainty. She is being asked to trust God in the absence of answers. How do you relate? Write out a prayer, in response, to him.

THINK

> *May the God of hope fill you with all joy and peace*
> *in believing, so that by the power of the Holy Spirit*
> *you may abound in hope. (Romans 15:13)*

1. When have you faced doubt and uncertainty in God's plans? Think of a specific instance or two.

2. Do you struggle in letting yourself dream? Do you ever believe you ask too much in asking God to fulfill your dreams?

3. What words did God say to Hannah that you most needed to hear?

 TRUST

Open a window. Or take a walk outside. Invite Jesus to be with you, showing you what he sees. Pay attention, yet rest. Let him hold your hand.

 PRAY

Father, give me faith to believe you, even in uncertainty. I give you my discontent. Show me how I struggle, how I ache, how I yearn for something I don't have right now. Thank you for the desire you give me for more of you. Thank you that you are right here. Everything I really need, I already have. Help me surrender my heart to you, trusting you and the good you always have for me. In Jesus' name, Amen.

Asphalt and Basketball and Home

THERE'S A HOLE IN MY SHOE where it scuffed too much. The rubber pulled off at the toe. I should have picked up some Shoe-Goo last night and fixed it. No big deal. These shoes will work tonight. Time to grab my ball and go.

Jesus, you know the cracks in the sidewalks, the hopscotch lines near the blacktop. The asphalt on the courts is uneven, roots from the trees pushing up the old tar. Got to pay attention or know where you're going. I know where I'm going, thanks to you. It took me a while to be able to say that, didn't it?

A chain link fence circles the court. Michelle's inside. She's got a group of girls and a few boys surrounding her, deciding teams. They're dividing up, so there's a mix of boys and girls on each side. Making it fair, as best she can. Chain links stretch up, keeping balls and twelve-year-olds mostly inside. Yeah, I remember.

I pass by the courts on Tuesdays at four. I grew up on these streets. I didn't know my dad. Mom was around. Sometimes. My grandma was the solid one for me and my brother. Took us to church each Sunday. The night before, she'd braid my hair so tight I could barely see. I watched TV and prayed my hair wouldn't pull right off. But she was always so kind.

Her apartment is one block up from the courts. On Tuesdays I visit her. She's fine, though she can't see well now, and her hip aches. She won't use a cane. I go sit with her and she insists on cooking dinner. I stay until *Wheel of Fortune's* over, then take the bus back down to 121st, where I live now. Maybe a little safer, but it isn't home.

I brought my ball today. There's been something about seeing Michelle on the court that makes me feel strange inside. Because I was one of those girls on the blacktop. I remember how hard it was, my Grandma doing what she could so my world didn't feel too upside down. I spent a lot of time on the street, running this sidewalk, playing ball. In this neighborhood, you need to know who you are and what you're doing or you're going to get *stuck*. My dad got stuck. My mom got stuck too. I made lots of mistakes and got stuck for a while. I was convinced I'd be stuck for good, just like them.

But Grandma believed in me. She said I was smart. Said I just needed to trust you, Jesus, and you would be with me, that your love for me could get me out of any circumstance, no matter how bad. I heard her, but my heart didn't take it in yet. Things got worse—drinking turned to drugs turned to prostitution so I could get the drugs.

Then there was the night it all went down. I had no money. I knew I couldn't keep going the way I was. She took me in one more time, my grandma. I told her I had to believe her, believe all that she said about you. I knew one thing: I was going to die if I didn't start believing.

It was hard, God; you know how hard. But life changed.

You tell me it takes courage. You say it takes faith to be strong. Well, in the Bible you tell me we don't even have to be strong, because *you* are strong. But we need faith. And you give that to me, Jesus. You keep giving me faith and love and hope.

Michelle sees me go by each Tuesday. She yells "Hey!" and asks me to come in and play—she can use another set of hands. I keep telling her no—"I've got to see my Grandma."

You're in there too, I guess, high-fiving Michelle and those kids. I see you there, smiling and loving on them like you do. You must have had your arms around me, just like that, when I was young, and I didn't even know it. I bet you're good with a basketball. I've got it in my mind to tell these kids about you. I want to make sure they know they're not alone and you love them and they've got a good future ahead, a plan for them.

Yes, you do.

Yeah, Jesus, I hear you.

I'll play today.

YOU'VE LIVED LIKE AN ORPHAN, girl. And no one could blame you. You've wandered and looked for home, scuffed shoes, soles peeling right when you needed to depend on them. It hasn't been fine. It hasn't been fair. You've gotten knocked down, laid out on that blacktop more than once. But look at your grit.

You're something.

And now you're finding home.

This strength in you is me. For my Spirit fills you. You don't remember this, but I remind you now: You know when you were in church one day, ten years old, and you asked me to come into your heart? I did, Laura. My Spirit came into your heart, and you knew me. You loved me—the love of a child—and that was the first step of faith. And now you're grown, a woman, and you love me even more than you did then.

You left for a while. My heart broke for you. I looked, awaiting your return each day. I never left you, not in the haze, not under the neon, not in the by-the-hour motels. I was your true Father, waiting for your heart to turn for home. And when you did, my Laura? My feet pounded the pavement, running to you, shouting, waking up the neighborhood at midnight, yelling that you were back. She's *back*, *Laura's* back, she's *back*.

You're back.

Yes, go on in through the chain links to those kids. When you're with the children, be asking me, in your heart, how to love them well. You know it, but I'll teach you. You've seen it, but I'll show you. It'll be fun.

You'll work hard in the paint, drive for the basket, lay it up, nothing-but-that-mother-loving-net, show the kids how to fake it, pivot on a heel—even though the shoe tears. You'll show them how to play what they've got. And you'll show them how, with me, you've got everything. Forever. Now.

I rejoice in you.

 LISTEN

Laura returns to the same streets where she grew up, a neighborhood where she faced a challenging childhood and made tough choices as a young adult. God has restored her to him, and she wants to love, in his name, the people he brings into her life. What do you think about this conversation between Laura and God? Write a prayer in response.

THINK

> *But while he was still a long way off, his father saw him and*
> *felt compassion, and ran and embraced him and kissed him. . . .*
> *"My son was dead, and is alive again; he was lost, and is found."*
> *And they began to celebrate. (Luke 15:20–24)*

1. What were the circumstances of you accepting Jesus? How have your life experiences–including where you grew up–shaped your faith?

2. God tells Laura, "Welcome home." How have you ever left God? What are the details? How would you describe your return?

3. How has God redeemed your mistakes? How has he given you another chance at life with him?

4. What, in his response to Laura, did you most need to hear God say to you?

 TRUST

Read Luke 15:11–32, the Parable of the Prodigal Son. Ask God to show you the character with whom you most identify. Can you relate to the younger brother who squandered all he was given and returned home? Is what the father tells the older brother something you need to hear? Ask God to search your heart and reveal to you what he has for you, what he wants to tell you about your heart, your past, mistakes you've made he wants to redeem, and the head-over-heels love he has when you return to his arms and want to be home.

 PRAY

Father, your love is scandalous and beautiful. You look for me when I leave. And you come running when you see me turn toward you. I don't deserve your love, yet I am desperate for it. I am desperate for you. Sometimes I know when I've turned away from you, and sometimes I don't. Help me see how you invite me home, how I've run away and how you invite me to return. In Jesus' name, Amen.

What the Heart Knows

GOD, THIS IS STUPID, TALKING like you can hear me. You aren't here. You don't see me. You don't love me or care about me. All those pleas in the night. You didn't make him stop coming, night after night.

I lay in my bed as still as I could, facing the wall. I kept my arm tucked under my head, my knees pulled up, my nightgown pulled down. I tried to will myself to sleep. My stuffed animals looked at me, the crowd of them lined up to protect me from the ghosts that lived in the wall, ghosts that looked like shadows from the streetlamp outside, ghosts that prowled in the night and could reach me if the bedroom wall's cold plaster had contact with my skin. I was six.

The door didn't even creak when he opened it. He was almost silent when he walked in. A slight shuffle, one step and then two, a bare foot treading on beige carpet. I would hold my breath then, telling myself I was no longer there. My stuffed animals couldn't protect me, and you couldn't either—not from darkness or from ghosts or from the roughness of his hands.

If I were dead, I imagined, I wouldn't need protection. Maybe that is why you didn't come and protect me. Maybe that is what made it so easy for me to believe, when he came in the night all those years, I was already dead.

I didn't believe in you then any more than I do now. But the counselors here tell me you are a good God, that sometimes bad things happen and we can't explain it. So I guess I'm never going to know why you didn't protect me? I'm supposed to just be okay with you letting a little girl get raped almost every night for eight years? Really, God? What kind of God are you?

You're jacked. That's what kind. This whole thing where I come and try to deal with my feelings? It's messed up—the people here are a joke. They act like they know. But they don't. They tell me talking it out will help me heal, that believing in some higher power, like you, will help take the focus off of myself and help me get on with my life.

Yeah, *get on with my life*. I am waiting for my life to start.

I am no good.

Maybe that is why you didn't come?

Whatever you are, whoever you are, I don't think you're a good God. I don't think you are "mighty" or "strong" or "loving." Whatever. If you weren't there, you didn't care. If you were, that makes it worse.

I am only writing this because the counselors made me do it.

I'm strong now. I'm fine now. I'd like to see anyone try to hurt me now.

If you're even real, you were never there, and you're not here now, and I hate that they make me write letters to you.

Whatever.

MY DAUGHTER, stand up. I have made you with strength. I have made you with a spirit of fierceness. You are not weak, and never were. You are not the one I forgot or turned my back on. You are not the one I don't love. You are not the one I don't want. I adore you. I never wished evil for you. I am your Father who gives to his children. What I have is yours. But there is darkness in this world. And a battle wages against it, in my Son's name. I will not explain now so you will understand. Will you believe in me even though you don't have all the answers, the reasons *this* happened and *that*?

I hate what happened to you. My fury knows no limit. I shall become a consuming fire for you, for all vengeance is mine, justice is in my hand, and my eyes are in every place, keeping watch on the evil and the good.

My justice is perfect, an edge of glittering diamond. It would be better for him to have a millstone tied about his neck, and to be cast into the sea.

But that is *him*. You are *you*. Will you give me your burden?

You want to understand. To know "why." If I am Almighty, why did I not protect you? "Where were you when he hurt me? Where were you when I asked you to save me and you didn't? How can you say you love me when you don't protect me?" I hear you. I will answer those one day. Listen now.

I will speak for you and your whole kind, ask questions harder than yours. Where was I at Wounded Knee? Where was I in the ovens of Auschwitz? Where was I on the red fields of Cambodia? Where was I in Nagasaki and Hiroshima? Where was I in Baghdad, in Kabul, in Aleppo? Where was I in the hundred million rapes of the world, the thousand million murders, the million million slaveries and injustices? Where am I in the blood, the cruelty, the screams, the sobs, the silence of corpses and the tears of the ravaged?

Where am I? Where am I? Where am I?

How can I? How can I? How can I?

You will know in time.

Now is the season for trust, the day of the whirlwind. I am bringing restoration.

I am more than what you see. I am more than what you feel. I am more than explanations. I am more than expectations.

I am. I am. I am.

You are my daughter, my true heir. Stand. Believe that. Your heart knows the answer your mind rejects.

We shall crush darkness into light.

Together.

 **LISTEN**

Jacqueline is not sure God is even listening. She is not sure he has been present in her deepest pain. What feelings do you wrestle with when you hear Jacqueline's words to God? What do you want to say to God in response?

_____

_____

_____

_____

_____

_____

_____

_____

_____

_____

_____

_____

_____

_____

_____

_____

_____

_____

_____

_____

THINK

He will wipe away every tear from their eyes,
and death shall be no more, neither shall there be mourning,
nor crying, nor pain anymore, for the former things
have passed away. (Revelation 21:4)

1. Have you ever had difficulty believing something the Bible says about God? Have you ever doubted his goodness, his presence? Is there anything God has said to you—or someone has told you about him—that is difficult for you to believe?

2. How would you respond to God's response to Jacqueline? What question does he ask her that you find the most challenging? Or what did you, personally, most need to hear?

 TRUST

Have you ever asked God where he was in a situation in your life, one that caused you terrible pain? Is there a moment, a point in your life, where you feel like he was not there? Right now . . . ask him into that place. Stay. Listen. Wait for him to show up.

PRAY

Father, bring healing to the broken places in my heart. Show me how to trust you. Bring people around me, community who knows me and loves me, to guide me toward a deeper relationship with you. Show me how to love you, especially when there are things I can't reconcile, things I don't understand. Show me how you are safe and you are good and that you can bring restoration and hope, even when all hope feels lost. Show me where you are now, with me. Let me see your face. I am desperate for you, Father. Please come. In Jesus' name, Amen.

You are more than what you can see:
You are light shining bright, my love.
You are my daughter in rays of sunshine,
even when skies are dark all around
and the storm's rains are pouring fast.
You do not have to be strong.

Whole

THE BLUE SQUARE TILES ARE SMOOTH, cool against my palms. I press down hard, fingers grasping the edge of the kitchen counter, asking you, please, make this room stop spinning. The second hand on the clock ticks like a bomb about to explode. It is quiet in the house, our youngest not yet up. I want to stop standing here, my hands gripping these bright cold tiles. I want to stop wondering why, God, you feel so far away.

I open the back door and step outside, cold cement under my bare feet. I don't know, God, if I've ever felt free. When I've let friends pray for me you've shown me myself as a little girl, a girl in a white dress, the wind blowing back her hair as she laughed and let herself run and jump and play. I'm not sure why you show me her. I see her face, the round cheeks and bright eyes of a young girl who only looks a little like me. When you look at me, is this really what you see?

It's hard to believe. All I know for sure right now is that my stomach aches. All I know for sure right now is that this little girl can't possibly be me. I try to see her, but I can't see her. Not really. It's not that I've forgotten her; it's that I doubt the little girl with the bright smile ever existed. I doubt she was ever part of me. How can I accept what you see?

I don't want to accept it. I don't want to believe you. You show me that little girl, but I can't accept her. All I can see is pain, regret, the image of my sister, on the freeway, dying, those cars going by so fast. There are awful things happening in this world, God, and you say you want to heal me, be with me, love me? Aren't there other things you should be worrying about right now?

Do other people feel this way? I'm struggling with so many tangled feelings. The only word for it is "broken." Am I broken, God? Is that what this comes down to?

I'm such a mess, God. How do I let go of this pain and hear you and see you and know, without a doubt, that I am yours? How can I possibly be fully yours when I feel broken and so alone? Are you here to save?

LET ME comfort you. I know it is hard to hear me when you doubt I was with you when you needed me most. Because it was earlier than your sister's death that you needed me. It was earlier than the night she died when you cried out, pleading for rescue. I have been there the whole time.

Yes, you are broken. All people are. And no, you are not broken. No one is.

You are not alone. And I can make you whole again.

I know you feel shattered in a million pieces. You want to collect them, offer them up, but you don't feel like they are worth much. So when you hear the word "surrender," you aren't sure it will do any good. You don't believe your life is one worth surrendering. You don't believe I've come for you. You don't believe you are cherished and perfectly beautiful and you shine, my daughter, you shine.

Do you know what I love to call you, in the night, when your mind is racing and you want to know—oh, you want to know—why this happened, and how this happened, and when the pain will ever stop?

I call you my Cherished One. I reach out my hand and brush away your tears, and I cradle you. For you are still that little girl inside, you know, my darling. And that is good. It is not bad that you feel fragile. It is okay that you don't feel whole. Keep looking to me for wholeness. Keep looking to me for all the broken pieces to be gathered, made beautiful.

I am whole. And what I am, I make you to become.

 **LISTEN**

Kate is convinced she is broken, a mess. She is overwhelmed and in pain. What is your reaction to Kate and what she shares, in prayer, with God? Can you relate to any of Kate's emotions or questions to God? Write your prayer to God in response.

THINK

> *To you, O Lᴏʀᴅ, I lift up my soul.*
> *O my God, in you I trust;*
> *let me not be put to shame;*
> *let not my enemies exult over me . . .*
> *Make me to know your ways, O Lᴏʀᴅ;*
> *teach me your paths.*
> *Lead me in your truth and teach me,*
> *for you are the God of my salvation;*
> *for you I wait all the day long. (Psalm 25:1–5)*

1. Have you ever doubted God's goodness? When has it been the most difficult for you to believe God's love for you?

2. How are you, right now, most challenged to trust God?

3. What part of God's response to Kate did you need to hear, too?

4. How is God inviting you into wholeness—restoration, healing—with him?

 TRUST

Close your eyes. Open your hands. Trust that God is here. Ask him to come and (1) show you himself, (2) tell you how he sees you, and (3) reveal what healing he wants to do in you to bring you his wholeness. Stay here. Wait on him. Let it sink in: *You are so loved by God.* And he has promised to make us whole.

 PRAY

Father, I can withstand anything when I know you are by my side. I give you all my pain, my doubt, the memories I wish I could change. You are sovereign, the Alpha and the Omega, the beginning and the end. Help me trust you, knowing there will always be so many things I don't understand. Help me believe this: I am yours; you are for me; your love for me is in me and will sustain me, in the highest waters, the darkest storms. I am your daughter. Let me feel you holding me close. In Jesus' name, Amen.

2:00 a.m. and Desire

IT'S TWO O'CLOCK IN THE MORNING. I gather my baby boy from his crib before his cries wake his dad. We slip into the kitchen. The stacked dishes are about to topple, a heap next to a row of bottles lined by the breast pump on the counter. Sweet one, oh, how you exhaust me, but I love you so.

Street lamps behind our little house shine through the living room sliding glass doors. Enough light to see my baby's face, his sleepy eyes scrunched tight, his tiny fingers waving the air to an invisible orchestra until I swaddle him tighter in the blue blanket and tuck him up next to me, close.

There you go, little one. You hungry?

He is beautiful, his seven-week-old body strong and determined. I ease into the blue striped chair and invite him to eat, his fingers in a fist now, pushing into my chest, his pink cheeks angled toward me. I will myself to stay awake. Father, help me. Help me keep him safe. Are you here, holding me, too?

It's been cloudy here. The dim glare from the street lamps makes it impossible to see any stars even if it wasn't. Oh, God, this heart of mine is unsure of what it feels. I am tired, numb, and stumbling. Will you lead me back home? Will you show me where you are? I fear this heart of mine is asleep for too many moments. I fear I am complacent, forgetting to look for you in the soft and quiet peace of these days. Will you help me find my way back to you?

I miss you.

I close my eyes. Just a few minutes? I want to imagine you.

There.

There is color all around, bright blues and gold and green. I step into it, arms outstretched, barefoot in grass. Then I'm running, hair blowing back. I jog up the hill and lie back into pillows of scented moss, foxglove, and columbine. Birds sing, and trees play music all their own—leaves tinkling like gold pieces in sun. It's the aspens I love most, their trunks stretching up like sentries, their fingers reaching to heaven. Yes, there is life here.

I lie down in the grass and watch the clouds, the puffs of white drifting like dandelion fluff through sky of cotton-candy blue. Your sun, God, covers me like a blanket. I close my eyes, your shoulder my pillow, your beating heart a lullaby. I am sleeping. I am awake.

I love how I can turn to you with my desire for more of you, and you awake me to beauty—yes, beauty in the place where we go together in my imagination, but also the beauty of what is right in front of me. Yes, there's a mess on the counter; yes, my wrists ache from days of holding my newborn and lifting my two-year-old out of her crib; yes, I haven't showered in two days and my hair is tangled in its bun. But my desperation for you is sweet, Father.

From my desire of you, help me awake. I want to feel freedom, God.

Sweet baby. You've fallen asleep. Let's get you back into bed, all snug and warm, my love.

With one arm keeping him tucked in close, I use my other arm to ease myself up, out of the deep cushions of the chair. My bare feet step carefully to his bedroom. It's dark, the shades pulled down. I bend down and lay his warm, relaxed little body into the crib. *Yes, sleep, dear one.*

Father, help me awake.

MY BRIGHT SHINING ONE, there is color all around you. You radiate hope. You emanate me.

I see you. I know you. You are given rest. You are loved and not forgotten. You are found and held.

You are my darling one who speaks healing with her words. You are my song, my *poemia*, my making, my beauty who lets me show you how special you are, in my name.

My lovely one, close your eyes now. For I *am* here, in the long days. I *am* here, in the uncertainty. I *am* here, in the exhaustion. I *am* here, in the wondering of what's next and when and how.

Those children you hold? That husband you commit to? They are mine. I give you new eyes to believe in what you can't readily see—the promise of my life in you, the good plan I have for you and for all the children I call my own. Come now, I create you. What I create is not mundane.

My love is what sustains you. My love awakens you to remember me, even when you feel so distracted—weary, complacent, forgetful of me. You can easily convince yourself you are missing me. But I meet you right here. Even right here. Reject the lie that you are far from me, Ruby.

I am here, in your desire of me. Awake now.

I see you in your glory. Step in deeper now.

I restore you. Receive freedom now.

I silence the lie that the moments at the sink washing dishes, or in the bedroom cleaning a child, or in the night feeding a baby, or in the home loving your husband mean you are sleeping, that you are not awake to your life, that your life is mundane. All work is holy work when you see me in it.

No, you are not missing me.

Love is never mundane.

 LISTEN

Ruby is awaking to how the restoration she experiences by being in God's presence fuels her love for her family and other people God will bring into her life. Close your eyes. Imagine you are sitting in the dark with God one sleepless night. What does God have to say to you? How does he invite you to love? Write down your prayer to God in response.

_____

_____

_____

_____

_____

_____

_____

_____

_____

_____

_____

_____

_____

_____

_____

_____

_____

_____

_____

_____

_____

 THINK

> *Taking her by the hand he said to her, "Talitha cumi,"*
> *which means, "Little girl, I say to you, arise." (Mark 5:41)*

1. What is it about Ruby that grabs your attention? What stirs your heart about her?

2. How are you longing for more of God?

3. How are you asleep to your desire for God? How do you need God to show up and awaken your desire for him?

 TRUST

Read Mark 5:35–43. Lie down in a comfy spot, where it is quiet and no one will disturb you for a few moments. (If you're a mom with young kids, I understand this is a challenge!) Once you've read the passage and are lying down, imagine you were once dead, but Jesus leans over you, pronounces you alive, says you are only sleeping, and asks you to rise.

Ask God about the ways you have been sleeping in your life. How have you become complacent? How have you been too timid? Ask him what desires he has placed in your heart, what new things he has for you.

Now imagine Jesus speaking directly to you. Listen to him say, "_____ arise," and open your eyes. Write down the ways you have been asleep and the ways God is inviting you to awake to the full life he has for you.

 PRAY

Father, wake me up. I don't want to sleepwalk, missing you in the simple moments of my life. Show me how I have been unaware of your presence in me. Awaken me to identity in you; make me hungry for the desires you place in my heart. Show me how I can experience you, uniquely, in my work, my relationships, my choices in my life. Show me how I can experience you everywhere. You have more for me than I can imagine. And I want to trust you and pursue you with my whole life. I'll no longer go only halfway. This is the life you've given me. Help me to want to experience you in all of it. I pray your promise, "Delight yourself in the Lord, and he will give you the desires of your heart" (Psalm 37:4). Amen.

LEA

Room

THE SCRAPBOOK IS PUSHED TO THE BACK, behind the candles and the tablecloths Mom uses for Christmas. Grainy Instamatic dreams on cardstock, photo corners holding them in place, in time. A little girl smiling. Digging at the beach. Dancing in her nightgown. Blowing out candles. Posing in a ruffled dress in front of a lighted Christmas tree. It looks so good. And she was happy for so many of those days, I think. There are fewer photos as she grew, before she secured herself a passport and packed up two suitcases and stepped onto a plane and went away.

Which is the real story? What is true—the story of the girl before she left or the one after she got back?

The white space in the middle, the years the scrapbook doesn't record, is what hurts the most. She had nothing but space, silence, room.

There are no pictures of her when she returned, or of the months when she was gone and she cried herself to sleep. There are no photos of her when she stopped eating. There are no photos of the girl who returned at sixteen, her body a representation of all that was broken—the worn out little girl who wanted to fix all the broken parts in her life, parts she found she couldn't fix on her own, or control.

I don't want to remember her.

For one year she was gone—thousands of miles to a different continent where she couldn't speak the language or be with anyone she knew. Her parents didn't know how she was really gone years before, how something, for so long, had needed to change. She needed to feel seen, and instead, she tried to disappear. That's the cost, I guess, for trying to repair something you can't, for trying to control something you can't.

What does it take, God, for a mom and a dad to see a little girl? What does it take for a voice—a voice calling out as loud as I knew how—to be heard?

I wanted to see if they cared if I left. Or maybe I wanted to see if I could hurt them a bit. I hated the discord that never seemed to ebb, even in my dreams at night.

I don't like to think about her—the girl who didn't know where she fit, the girl who didn't know why things felt so out of control. I don't want you show me where you were in those moments when I felt so forgotten. I don't want you speak to me about the moments when I felt alone and it seemed like no one cared I was there. Until I left.

God, I am afraid to remember her. I am afraid to see her again. I am afraid to know what you see when you look at her, when you look at me even now.

MY DAUGHTER, DO YOU KNOW there is laughter inside you, even here? I love to listen to it, even when you can't hear it. I gave you such a smile—magnetic. You captivate me, and I hold your hand, and

I love how we get to be together these days. I have been with you all the days, my love. I see you.

Are you asking me to show you what I see in you? Now or then? It doesn't change, you know.

I made you determined. I made you carefree. Joy-filled, too. Have you forgotten? Your strength is practiced. You've chosen it when you've felt there was no one else to be strong. You chose control when you felt there was no one else to direct the chaos. You let your heart harden when you felt love wasn't for you, and you thought you had to make things happen on your own.

You have spent your life choosing things—a way of looking at the world that has made you carry burdens. You were never meant to carry those burdens, my child. I have been here, waiting for you to give them to me.

True strength is surrendered pride. True strength is humbleness, faith. True strength is not pretending you are stronger on your own, without me leading the way.

I know you felt scared and overwhelmed. You made a decision, long ago, to not be weak anymore. You determined to be strong. You chose to count on yourself. You would depend on you.

It's been a long road since then.

Are you ready? Are you ready, now, to give each of those burdens to me? Can you give me your heart, now, even *now*? Can you give me that moment when the world around you closed in and you chose to stop eating? Can you give me that moment when all felt dark and you felt you couldn't find your way out? Can you give me that moment when you were in your room and you decided, right then, to not be weak anymore?

Can I be your strong one now? Can I come in and show you a new way of looking at this life?

There can be another snapshot. Our moment that will never end.

 **LISTEN**

Close your eyes. Imagine Lea. See her and her Father before her, bending low and sharing what he sees. What is it you hear him saying to you? Write your own prayer back to God.

 THINK

Do not be anxious about anything, but in everything
by prayer and supplication with thanksgiving let your
requests be made known to God. (Philippians 4:6)

1. Can you relate to Lea's struggle with control? How have you ever tried to change yourself when circumstances around you were not what you hoped?

2. In what situations do you find it most difficult to let go? When is it hardest to keep from trying to control things on your own?

3. When do you feel most anxious and alone and unloved? In those moments, how can you let God come in and care for you heart?

 TRUST

You can do this exercise alone. But better yet, you can do it with a trusted friend who loves God and loves listening to him. In prayer, confess your broken heart; confess to God a specific experience in your past that you have difficulty accepting. Consider a moment, whether recent or in the past, that hurt deeply. Imagine yourself in that moment. Imagine yourself in that situation, even though you might not want to, even though it's quite uncomfortable.

Put yourself back there and talk to God about what it feels like. Tell him all the things you wish were different, all the ways you hurt and wish it never happened. Stay there. Then ask God to show you where he is in this moment. Ask the Holy Spirit to show you Jesus in the place, in the experience. What is he doing? What does he see that you do not? What does he say to you? How does he rewrite the story and bring healing to your past, creating you brand new? Finally, how do you respond to him?

PRAY

Father, crush every lie I've believed. Crush every fear to which I've succumbed. I give you my heart. I give you my pride—my desire to control, to change things I cannot. I trust you to give me strength and faith to follow you and change the things I can. I know you are with me. I know you never leave me. I know your plans are good, and I know you can bring me peace. Thank you for how you give me new eyes to see my story. Thank you for how you rewrite it, how you give me a fresh start, a new life. You are my God, and you are my hope, and your Holy Spirit lives in me. I believe in your truth more than in anything else. In Jesus' name. Amen.

Behind Elevator Doors

SIX O'CLOCK. FLOOR 40. ELEVATOR packed. I step in, bag over my shoulder, black pumps digging into my heels. I readjust the bag stuffed with files, edits to the documents we've been working on for months. I squeeze in on the left side of the moving matchbox, making the obligatory about-face turn to face the just-closing elevator door. I'm wedged between a guy with a silver-blue tie and a twenty-five-ish-year-old woman with black curls, clutching a bag even bigger than mine. Deep breath. Not too deep, though, in this tiny space. I slouch my shoulders forward, lowering my bag from hip to knees, trying to make more room. Against the pull of the strap and against my tired muscles, I look up. Thirty-nine more floors. Thirty-eight. *Sigh.*

Today was good. I made eye contact with Mandy and Ryan during my presentation. They had no *idea* how nervous I really was. It feels great to get out of here early after staying so late last night—getting all my stats together, tweaking the slides so they were clear. Sodden tea bags piled up next to that cruel half-pound bag of M&M's until I waved the white flag at one o'clock.

Right before I walked into the conference room, I took that deep breath, asking you to come, too, and you did. You calmed me. You helped me breathe. I could almost see you sitting across the table, looking at me. That's what did it—what allowed me to speak clearly and not falter or grasp for words during one of the most crucial presentations I've ever given. You. Looking at me. Your love is crazy, you know that? It was such a simple thing, but you cared for me the way I needed in that moment.

Ding. The doors slide open. The guy in the suit steps out. Twenty-eight.

Your constant love and presence astounds me. What's it like for you, I wonder, crowded in this stuffy elevator with us? I know you are here. And your love doesn't mind it. I bet you don't feel awkward, or impatient, or tired—instead, you support the ones who do, lifting up our weary heads. You know these tired faces; you've been holding us together all day: "I'm here, I know it's hard, I've got you." Twenty more floors. Nineteen.

I'm gonna close my eyes. Do you mind? I picture in my mind the facets of your love—you are my Creator, my Redeemer, my King, my Bridegroom. You are the one who wrapped a towel around your waist and bent gently to wash the feet of your friends. You have always done this, haven't you? Given yourself the way that we needed you. Fifteen.

You are so beautiful, holding me up, holding us all up. Your strong hands under ours, under mine. Thirteen.

You bend still, leaning down over me. I feel your breath above me. Twelve.

How do you bend so low, my Lord? How did you do it then? Your body broken? Your skin flayed wide? Blood runs down your face, your hands, your side. You carried your cross, dragging the weight of the world. You carry it and carry me, too. Eight.

Let me take off these shoes. Let me put down this bag. Let me stay here, at your feet. Let me say thank you. Wash my feet—and my head, and all of me. Keep me here, in your place of love, love that transforms this place into our home. Three.

Oh, my Lord. One. How do you stay?

I LOVE HOLDING YOU.

It is my joy to be the Great Servant of all, the Great Lover of all. To belong to all, yet still be yours alone.

Any space is ours, our home and shelter. The meeting room, filled with your nervous energy, this elevator crammed with others. I can find you anywhere. I follow you, and I lead you, and I teach you how to follow while I lead. It is beautiful. You are beautiful.

Keep your eyes closed. Can you see it? Can you hear it? I know you can. You are surrounded by love. You are surrounded by beauty— and joy—even here. You are surrounded by voices raised in singing, souls lifted up, dancing. It is time to worship, my dear, as I wash your feet, now and evermore.

Stand tall now. Raise your hands. Lift your voice, your whole soul singing out. You can't help but do it. You are made to serve and be served, to dance with God. You are made to be completely with me. This is what restores you, heals you, fills you so love overflows from your whole self.

Ask me for myself. It is not too much.

But I shall ask for you in return.

There is no such thing as half of love.

 LISTEN

Can you visualize yourself in the place of Bridget, present with Jesus in the elevator? Is this easy to do, or difficult? What is your response to this conversation? Write your prayer to God.

THINK

*For this reason I bow my knees before the Father, from whom every family
in heaven and on earth is named, that according to the riches of his glory
he may grant you to be strengthened with power through his Spirit in your
inner being, so that Christ may dwell in your hearts through faith–that you,
being rooted and grounded in love, may have strength to comprehend
with all the saints what is the breadth and length and height and depth,
and to know the love of Christ that surpasses knowledge, that you
may be filled with all the fullness of God. (Ephesians 3:14-19)*

1. How do you feel about the way Jesus showed up for Bridget during her presentation? Do you agree with her–that Jesus is crazy in how he loves? Or do you struggle to believe this is true for you in your own life?

2. How have you experienced Jesus loving you in the last few days? Where have you seen him show up for you most recently?

3. What is your reaction to Jesus inviting Bridget to give all of herself in response to him giving everything?

TRUST

Where do you *feel* the presence of God? Go to that place, do that thing, with care and intention. Picture the ways he gives himself for you. Ask him how you can give yourself, fully present, in return.

PRAY

Jesus, remove my hesitation to be present with you. Help me want to experience your closeness; help me want to worship you without reservation. Help me enter into your presence and receive your grace–your Spirit filling me with your joy, hope, and peace. Let me live in this sacred space with you, no matter where I am. Help me practice worshipping you in all situations, in all places. Let me fall more deeply in love with you. In your name I pray, Amen.

Mountains and Bedroom Windows

THE ROOM IS DARK, THICK cotton curtains pulled across my window. The outside sill is powdered with pollen from the spring-time trees. I stuff the down pillow farther under my head and tug the white coverlet over my arms. What time is it? Oh, Father, I don't want to know. Actually, I don't care.

Is this the bottom? Can I sink deeper? I am too tired to talk, especially to you.

Bottles of pills, dust-covered books. I need it quiet, God. I'm just going to squeeze my eyes tight now, turn the fan up a little higher. There, now I can no longer hear.

Let me stay in the darkness, in the quiet. I can't get up. I can't. I can't. I. Can't.

No, nothing can fix this, fix me. But I need to be different. This is not how it was supposed to be. What's wrong with me? Why won't this darkness lift?

Maybe I can't fix this, God. Maybe I can't keep running from you. I don't know what to do. I don't know how to escape. Please. Heal me. Please. Fix me. Please. Come. Just. Come.

There is memory I can't believe. Another girl. A different me. Who was she? Who was that girl? When did the darkness fall? How can she find her way out of it?

I am alone, in a forgotten place. A place with no doors and no windows. It is heavy, pressing in on all sides. Only memory of something different, a possibility I can't trust. Can I believe it? Memory of, maybe, hope.

But I look at her now, and I can barely stand it. She is despicable, God. She is ugly and worn and still young. She used to be strong, with a purpose, following a beacon ahead. She used to get excited about things, hope-filled. You could give her a challenge and she would rise to it. Oh, God, how can she rise now? She can't. Can she?

Help her, Father. Help her stand. Help her lift her head. Help her find her way out of this darkness. She can't stay here much longer. She can't stay. Oh, help her. She can't stay.

MY DEAR ONE, I HOLD YOU close now. Feel my heartbeat. That's it. Just there. Lean your head against my chest. Just stay. Let us stay here a little while. I wrap my arms around you, my precious one, my delight, my dearest heart whom I never want to let go. I don't. I don't let you go. I never have. I never will.

Daughter, you don't have to rise to see me. You don't have to be strong to be with me. You don't need to be healed to leave this bed and feel my light shine on you.

I am your shield. I am your compass. I am your resting place. I am your blanket who covers you. Do you feel me all around you? May I be with you? I don't think words are what you need now. You need to believe in something that goes deeper than what any words can tell you. You need to look inside yourself and see me there. You need to be shown what happens when the eyes of one's heart truly see.

With these eyes, she sees darkness around her but is blind to it, too, because of my light. She feels darkness pressing in, tangibly—her skin aching from what sadness feels like in a heart—but yet she sees my face. The eyes of her heart are looking in my eyes. My eyes, ever on her, reassure her, comfort her, remind her it is okay to be sad.

I will one day take this from you—this sadness, this pain. I will one day take this from you—the room spinning and the air so thin you feel you can't breathe. Let me settle you. Let me be your air. Let me shine light down upon you. This place is temporary and there is hope. I have light and fresh air and new things just for you.

I am with you when you are sad. I never leave you. I am right here. Just let me hold you, and I will let the light in. Just let me stay.

You will get used to me. You will learn to trust me. You will let me heal the hard places, the aching thorns that pierce your heart and make it difficult to rise.

I pull out the thorns, and I help you rise. I touch the wounds, the burning gashes that fester and bleed unless you let me touch my hand upon them, unless you let me in.

I see that girl you see, and I rescue her. I see that dear one, the one you despise, and I love her, and I heal her. She is radiant and wild and strong. She rises and she stands. Her hair flows straight back in the wind, and she looks to the mountains, and she mounts the horse that comes from the cliffs, and she jumps on its back, and she rides. She rides into the mountains, and she knows who she is and where she goes. She goes forth, deeper into the places of darkness so that other sisters, whom she will soon know, can be rescued by my love, too. She has been rescued, so she rides the places where other daughters who are trapped and lost can see, and know there is a way.

Yes, yes, I will bring you home. Yes, yes, I will find you. Yes, yes, I will show you how, now, you are indeed found. It is a long road, healing. I am not saying you won't feel like giving up. But I am here. I have you.

You know there is light, even if you can't yet see it. It is beyond the darkness, despite the darkness. It has overcome the darkness. Step into that light. The darkness cannot bear it.

With me, you can bear anything, child.

LISTEN

Charlotte is depressed. She feels overwhelmed and alone. And God responds. How do you feel about this conversation? What is your prayer to God?

 THINK

> *Heal me, O LORD, and I shall be healed; save me,*
> *and I shall be saved, for you are my praise. (Jeremiah 17:14)*

1. What has been your darkest moment, when you've felt despair, when you've felt alone?

2. How do you need to be rescued? How are you desiring God to give you light, fresh air, and new things?

3. What situation or wound is God asking you to give him? How is he asking you to trust him, right now?

 TRUST

Get out a pen and find a piece of paper or a journal. Write down the best thing God could ever say to you. What do you most want to hear? Then write down the most wonderful thing God could dream up for you to do with your life.

Now surrender these words to him. Ask him what he thinks of them. Trust that he will speak. Wait for him. Write down what he says. Test it against Scripture. (Does this sound like him? Is this true to his character?) Hold it close.

PRAY

Father, when I am weary and overwhelmed, you come and carry me. I am not alone. You are my compass. You are my strength. You pull out the thorns in my heart, bind my wounds, and make me whole. With you, I am filled with joy and with courage. With you, I can walk forward, unafraid of what is ahead. You heal me, and guide me up into the mountains. I follow you. No looking back. In Jesus' name, Amen.

Stand tall now. Raise your hands.
Lift your voice, your whole soul singing out.
You can't help but do it. You are made to dance.
You are made to be completely with me.

Waking Sleep

DARK GRAY PAVEMENT STRETCHES OUT straight and boring. The coffee I grabbed from work is lukewarm now, and cars crowd this busy freeway on all sides. Dusk is falling and it'll be forty minutes before I get home. Turn the radio up. Grasp the steering wheel. Focus on the road.

I am weary, Father. The days are long, but I am grateful for the work I get to do with you. I so want my coworkers to see you in me, your calm in my chaos, your presence easing my worry. I can hear you, when I pause. I can see you, when I seek. But I forget you a lot, don't I? Am I doing what I'm supposed to be doing?

When I am with you, I know who I am and I am content—not restless, but still. But I struggle to stay with you in the long hours at work, and in the night when I am exhausted. I want to disappear then, open a magazine and see what things I can buy. Or I want to go shopping with girlfriends and leave the stress of everything behind. I use pornography sometimes, too, to distract—or a romance novel. The visuals, the story, overwhelm me, and I place myself in them. I forget you so easily then, and I admit I feel empty. I hate heeding the lie that whispers, *"Anywhere is better than this place."*

How do I stay with you—and not try to escape—in the middle of stress, in the middle of tough decisions, in the middle of weariness? I don't even give you a chance, do I?

Wake me up, Father. Help me not be complacent with this life you've given me.

DO YOU THINK you can ever escape from love? Do you think you can stay away from your home? I don't force my way into your heart. I pursue you, yes. But I don't push my way in. And you know this. You know what it is like to be with me and to look for me, yes.

Do you know how I love to watch you, no matter what you are doing? Do you know I have formed you, just like this, to move with grace? I fill you with grace. I fill you with me. Don't fret, my dear. Don't worry about the weariness and the disquiet and the restlessness you feel from the work I've given you to do. Practice looking for me during the day, when you are at work, just like you do when you are still, with me. For you know what it is like to be with me.

Know that I am present with you, my darling, even when it feels like I am far. In your work and in your play, there is no place I don't want to be with you. Don't focus only on doing your days right, whether or not you are doing a good job of seeing me or looking for me. Choose me by loving what I love. Choose me by continuing to seek me. Choose me by desiring to stay.

I am here.

I am with you.

But I am not like you.

I am bigger than you can know. I am more than strength, more than safety. I am all things. You know me, and I only want to show you more. It is good you miss me when you have gone away. It is good you recognize how your heart yearns for me. But ask me to quiet the fears. Ask me to touch my hand upon your heart and deafen you to thoughts of worry. And let me guard your heart, your eyes, your ears, your imagination, your mind. There are dangers that can turn your desire to escape weariness into an opportunity to run far away from me.

Be my daughter. Be my girl. Stay.

Stay awake.

 LISTEN

Close your eyes. Imagine Nichole in the car, her hands gripping the steering wheel. How does your heart respond to her? What does God want to say to you about Nichole's conversation? How can you relate? Write your prayer in response.

THINK

Have I not commanded you? Be strong and courageous.
Do not be frightened, and do not be dismayed, for the LORD
your God is with you wherever you go. (Joshua 1:9)

1. God gives us gifts of rest and restoration. The tricky thing is making sure the things that bring us rest and restoration don't become more important than God. How do you try to escape or seek comfort apart from God? What is it about that activity that keeps you returning to it? What, in general, triggers you to want to seek escape or comfort? When did you do that most recently?

2. When have you recently felt God was far away? When have you felt him close? How is he encouraging you to spend time with him?

3. Where do you fail to see God because you forget that his love is vast? How can you remember God through the things he has given you passion for, or in the work that he has called you to?

 TRUST

Deep breath now. Consider a situation today that would tend to make you stressed, anxious, lonely, weak, or insecure. Take a minute . . . can you picture it? Close your eyes. Imagine yourself in that situation. See yourself there. Let all the emotions come . . . now picture Jesus there next to you, actually standing next to you, in the room. Imagine his face, his posture. Listen to what he says to you. Write it down. Ask him to help you remember him today.

PRAY

Father, you hold me. You are near me. In all moments, in all trials I face, and in the regular, everyday moments too, you treasure me. I want to be with you. You have written my name in your book, and you have chosen me, your daughter. You call me beloved, dearly loved. I am yours. Guard my wandering heart and body and mind. In Jesus' name, Amen.

From the Periphery

I HEAR GIGGLES DOWNSTAIRS IN the kitchen, then questions about breakfast and bargaining for whose turn it is to take the dogs out. Voices carry up the wood stairway to my bedroom windows, open wide. *I'm coming.* I am hungry for a few more minutes, in the quiet, with you.

Books are stacked on the floor near my bed, spines suggesting so many ways to live a better life: *seek gentle rhythm, choose prayer, do scripture memorization, desire wisdom, get community.* There's a lot of truth in those pages, but you've been whispering there is more for me. A "more" that can't be satisfied by simply listening to worship music, devouring books about you, or attending Bible studies. I want *you.* I want *more.*

A restlessness grows in me. It started with a desire to see you, hear you. So, for days, weeks, months, I grasp the leather journal and silver pen on my nightstand, looping each word even and small. "Breathe." Yes, you are my breath. "Wait." Yes, I trust you are here and I will be patient with the changes you are making in me. "See." Yes, I choose to see you, the more of you that is present with me in the beautiful mundane of an ordinary day.

And in these moments, I am in the garden with you, breathing Eden. Knowing the perfection of your good love for your children. I see the daughter you see, the one you keep close and restore to you. Peace is in me, and then a restlessness that is pure, that is good. I am not distracted, pulled away. I want more of you, answering back the prayer you put in me.

Let's go.

When girlfriends come over Tuesday morning to pray and worship together like we do, we want to be bold. We feel you in the room.

Ask me. Ask me for more.

So we do.

There are Tuesdays we spend asking you our names, asking you to show us truth, what words we should adopt as the descriptions of our truest selves. There are Tuesdays we battle, using the blood of Christ to shed the lies of the enemy that rob us of freedom, that distract us from our true place by your side. There are Tuesdays we ask you what we love, how you restore us, how you have knit us to worship you in unique ways. These are Tuesdays we are expectant. We love you. We love how you come. Still you say it: *Ask me. Ask me for more.*

My heart beats fast, my face hot. I go first. My sisters gather around. A hand on my back, my shoulders, my knees. A warmth settles on me, blanketing me, my chest tightening. I can feel you close. My sisters' hands are hot. God, you're here. Whether I can see you, feel you, or not, I know you are here.

What is it, God? What is the more you have?

Three friends hear words in their hearts as they pray. Two friends see, in their minds, pictures of me with you. *You are free* is the whisper repeated. *You are free* is what I hear in my heart. My sisters spill truth over me: You are captivating, beauty. You are surrounded by color—flags, banner waving. You have gone ahead; you know the way; you return, in color and in light, in freedom and in joy, to lead. You stand before the sons and daughters of God—your brothers, your sisters—as a beacon of light and color. *Hold out your hands now. Hold out your hands. Yes, you have within you the map. Look, I place it in your hands.*

You invite me into more that I can't yet see, but you see it. "Glory to glory."

Yes, there you are. You in me.

Let's go.

I open my hands, holding fast to the map.

Go.

DAUGHTER, I LOVE HOW YOU STAND. Deep breath now, keep those hands open. Yes, I have chosen you, and yes, there is more for you. I love how you desire it, how you charge toward it. You stay with me, and you wait on me. You know my voice in you, and you know what I have for you is good.

Now when you go forward, when you accept the more for you I have, you need to stay close to me. You are saying yes to things you can't do on your own. So you will see me in new ways, experience me afresh. Your faith will increase, and you will walk in greater boldness and conviction. You will stand and not cower, knowing I give you every weapon you need to fight every battle I ask you to fight.

Are you ready?

Remember those flags and banners, daughter? That color all around you? Those are flags and banners of the battlefield. Those are the decorations of the assembled sons and daughters who follow. For yes, remember that when you ask for more, and you are bold and fearless in my name, it is because you trust that I am in you. You trust I've given you what you need to go into places you've never gone before. You trust the information on the map.

So in the midst of battle, keep talking to me, my dear one. When the wind is waving the banners high, keep talking to me. Do not try to hide from me the desires of your heart. Remember how I speak to you? Breathe. Wait. See. That is how you are equipped for battle. That is how you invite me to stay.

I am your breath. Wait on me, and believe I am here, with you, right now. See me looking at you this moment, and practice trusting I am your Father, your friend, your leader, your Mother Bird, your strength, your gentle one, your nurturer, your guide, your king, your soft place, your shelter, your shield, your haven, your rest, your sun, your air, your joy and peace and light and hope. I am what is true. I am the map.

I am what you can wonder about, but about whom you don't need to wonder. I am your completeness. I am the answer to all wondering—and the beginning of wondering, too. Breathe. Wait. See.

 **LISTEN**

Consider Catherine in her room with the windows open wide. How, like her, are you restless and hungry for more of God? What is it you want to say to him? Write a prayer to God, in response to his conversation with Catherine.

THINK

And we all, with unveiled face, beholding the glory of
the Lord, are being transformed into the same image from
one degree of glory to another. For this comes from
the Lord who is the Spirit. (2 Corinthians 3:18)

1. How do you hunger for God? Describe the relationship you have with him now. Is this the relationship with God your heart craves?

2. Can you relate to Catherine's hunger for a deeper, more intimate relationship with God? Have you ever longed for such a relationship but have been unsure how to get it?

3. What did you most appreciate God saying to Catherine? What did you, personally, need to hear?

4. What is the "more" you want God to invite you into, with him?

 TRUST

Find a piece of paper and a pen. Better yet, open your journal. Write the word "Breathe" and ask God to show you how he wants to be your breath. Listen. Wait. Write down ways you need to depend on him.

Write the word "Wait" and ask God how he is inviting you to be patient with the changes he is making in you. Listen. Wait. Write down words that describe how God sees you and the good plans you believe he has for you. Claim these good plans, based on the goodness of God and his love for you—even though you don't know all the details of what God is planning.

Write the word "See" and ask God to show you what he has for you in the extraordinary beauty of an ordinary day. Listen. Wait. Write down the picture you see of God with you, this moment, this day.

PRAY

Father, you are magnificent in your love. You are playful and good. You are jubilant and kind. You chase me. You love to be with me. You invite me in deeper, desiring me to experience all of you. And I want that. I want to be with you fully. I don't want anything to get in the way of seeing, hearing, and feeling you. Come, Jesus. Come, Holy Spirit. Come, my Father. Teach this daughter of yours what it means to cling to you. I want more of you. I want to trust you and follow you, without reservation. Let me be bold and strong and fierce, with you. In Jesus' precious name, Amen.

Blue and White and New

I PEEK MY HEAD INTO his room again.

It used to be a bright royal blue, his bed pushed against the far wall. I painted the room white last month. Boards online called the paint "warm white." I brushed on those first strokes of white at ten o'clock one night, covering up the once-bright blue. The windows were open wide to star-dotted indigo night, and the breeze blew straight in. The crickets chirped so loud, I decided to turn down the music blasting through my speakers and listen to that night's own music play.

We sold his bed on Craigslist and replaced it with a full-size, wrought iron bed. We replaced the orange and white striped comforter with a chenille bedspread and the quilt my grandmother made from old dresses and dishtowels. But I've kept the Legos on the window seat in the corner, the truck with semitrailer, the race car with the shiny metal motor and wheels that spin. I lean into the room, one foot in, one foot out, after the two other kids leave for school. I am battling with hope, struggling to believe in the possibility of feeling normal again.

I miss him, that boy of mine. He had to go so soon. He was so little, God. I don't understand why some families have to experience so much pain, while others seem to make it through unscathed. Is that true, that some of us experience more pain than others? Or do we each experience similar degrees of suffering over our lives, but just different kinds and at different times?

Why did he have to suffer, God? I miss him so much. I am overwhelmed by my grief. Oh, God, he was our son.

I know you know pain, God. Sometimes I wonder if I can bear this pain, if I can keep going—and I feel guilty about this when you have given us other children to love and raise. When you have never left my side.

Still, why do some people's children live long lives and others die? Why do some people not get sick and others suffer? Why do children die, and why do their parents live?

It's interesting how we use words so carefully to describe something terrible. We use words like "loss" and "trial" and "hardship"—words that feel like mere words. Nothing can explain the agony of a parent facing a child's death.

You brought him to us, you took him from us, and I know you have him. But I miss him. I miss holding him, God. I also miss how he smelled. And I miss the feeling of his skin on mine. I miss his voice and his smiles.

Oh, God, continue to heal this heart of mine. You have not given more than I can bear, I think. But I miss him, and I know he is with you. Please keep healing me. Please help me parent these other dear children well. Please keep me close.

Protect my heart.

BELOVED ONE: I never left him. I held him each day. I was with him before he was born. I was with him the day he breathed his first breath. I am with him, even still, beyond the moment he breathed his last. It isn't over, my darling. It has only begun.

Your heart, I know, feels like it will burst from sorrow some days. Your heart feels too heavy for you to rise, on some. But I made you, and I made him, too. I am with you, from the beginning to the end.

Know this too: With me there is no end. This suffering, this pain and stretch of time when life feels so long and so hard . . . there will come an end. I have come, restored you, and called you by name. You are mine.

The sorrow cuts. But I want you to know this, too: I know your smile, and I know how you love, and I love your questions and your yearning. I love your desires and your dreams. Those dreams of yours are ones I want you to give me. You are made to be with me, trusting me, letting yourself believe in what feels impossible because anything is possible with me. I have held you, in the hard moments, and I have never left you. I know his absence feels so much to bear, but you also know I've given you a strength that you recognize as mine, in you.

I give you faith. I give you hope. I give you the dreams, the searching. There is so much more I have for you, my daughter.

Come. See.

 **LISTEN**

Hope is asking God to heal her of her broken heart after losing her son. What does this make you think about and feel? What is your prayer to God?

 THINK

Not only that, but we rejoice in our sufferings,
knowing that suffering produces endurance, and endurance
produces character, and character produces hope, and hope does not
put us to shame, because God's love has been poured into our hearts
through the Holy Spirit who has been given to us. (Romans 5:3–5)

1. Hope wrestles with questions she just can't find the answers to on her own. She knows God is her safe place, and she gives him her grief and her pain, as well her questions about things that just don't make sense. What questions do you wrestle with and want to give to God?

2. What tragedies have you suffered in your life? How are you suffering now?

3. What words to Hope bring you the most encouragement? Or is there anything God says to Hope that you struggle to accept, or to believe?

 TRUST

Find a smooth stone that you can write on. Look at it carefully, notice its curves, bumps, design, and color. In God's conversation with Hope, he tells her how he knows her, how he sees her, how he is inviting her to dream. What dream do you have with God? Hold the stone in your hand and close your eyes. Ask God to give you a word for the dream he is inviting you to share with him. Write it down on the stone with a permanent marker and keep it close to you, where you can see it. Continue to ask God for courage to pursue him. Ask him to help you believe more in how he made you—and for help in realizing that dream.

PRAY

Father, I give you my heart, which aches with the pain of loss, sadness, and regret. Restore me to you so I can dream. I want to live in the freedom of knowing you hold me, hold everything, in all situations—and that with you, everything is beginning again. In Jesus' name, Amen.

On Being Brave

HE STUFFS THE BLACK MOLESKINE into the back pocket of his jeans like it's a tool of battle, some weapon of truth. He logs words to remember what is good, proof of you in the day. Steel hammer on nail, gray smoke of campfire, giggles of our son in his crib. He says.

He seizes the ballpoint pen like it's a sword—running through doubt, ingratitude, and fear. If he can see you in the small, he says, he can see you—trust you—in the big. The gleam of oak floor-boards through opened curtains, the whistle of coffee pot on gas stove, the curve of hip under sheets at night. He says.

Distraction and disruption pull him away from you, as well as insecurity and doubt. You answer prayers in the un-hurry, in the slow, and this is what he sees: the curl of leaf in wind whipping, the mirrored branches in water rippling, the arc of line casting into river flowing. You are in the earth, the air, the sky, the tangible and intangible. He says.

I watch him, emboldened by his practice of looking for you, pausing—intentionally choosing to see you in this busy, harried world. The world pulls him one way, and yet he plants his feet in your truth and he stands, sure. He seeks your majesty, and he finds it. He insists on it. He waits for it. He expects you to reveal yourself. And he recognizes you everywhere.

He writes down what he sees because it is *you* he wants to see. I watch him, and I want to look for you. He shares with me the pictures you show him, the friend guiding him in how to see.

I want to see you, too.

Then the storm, Father—the money gone, the once secure job falling through. The wind whips our faces, rain crying angry tears, wind howling. We are in the middle, God. The boat tips and rolls as the land beneath the waters shakes—and if you are in the waves, God, we pray we see light in this dark night.

The bank leaves another message—a person this time, not a computerized voice. We know things are serious. We can't pay the rent on the studio, the coupons at the grocery store don't help enough anymore. I contemplate selling my ring. He tells me not to, not yet.

He isn't in denial. He isn't scared, though I can see the worry in the way his brows frown over his eyes. He sees you, knowing this experience is difficult but that you are with us, too. Can I believe this—that you are here? Does faith in you, in the midst of storms, mean we are trusting you to help? How does being grateful help when I can't buy food to eat and we have no home to live in and we are without a plan?

God of earth and air and sky, bring shelter, safe harbor. I am not yet practiced at seeing you, in believing. My eyes weak, my faith wavering, I pray to see what my eyes cannot.

DAUGHTER, STAY in the boat. Hang on tight and let go, too. For I steer you, and I see you, and I point the only way safe, the only way home.

Look beyond the waves. Focus on what you know: I am more than any storm. I am more than wind and rain and waves and the unknown. I say. I am more than what you can ever see.

Keep counting moments toward me. Keep claiming words for love. Keep practicing how to see me, in the dark, when you can't see, when you fear I am far away and you worry you are lost and the light-house's beam could never shine so bright and so far in the dark. I say.

You watch John look for me, and you know how to look for me, too. Yes, you are scared. Yes, you are wondering how you are going to survive—tell your landlord you have to move out, get food from the food kitchen another week, keep your clothes clean so you're ready to interview for a new job. It's a lot. I know. Especially when there is no help you can see.

So look for me. You'll see me. You will recognize how I bring direction. You will recognize there is more than danger in this storm. You will see deeper, further. You will recognize the guide I bring to show you, in the midst of the storm, how to effectively cast the sail.

It's time to face the storm with me next to you now, daughter. It's time to surrender and not face it alone.

Together, let's trim the sail. With me, it's okay if the wind is blowing and the storm is raging. Let the waves rage. Let the wind blow, I say! Open your eyes to see me. You have what it takes. I see it in you.

Is it really dark here now, my love? Is the wind so loud you can't hear me? Is the night so dark you can't see me? Is the storm so great you can't find me?

There is more to every day than what your eyes can see.

I am your lighthouse. I shine in the night, in the storm, in the darkness where you think light could not. Look up now, my love. Look up and keep seeing.

You see.

Really, right now, you see.

 LISTEN

Tessa is afraid, overwhelmed by circumstances she feels she can't control; yet she wants to be grateful to God in all circumstances. What is your prayer to God?

THINK

> *And as they sailed he fell asleep. And a windstorm came down*
> *on the lake, and they were filling with water and were in danger.*
> *And they went and woke him, saying, "Master, Master, we are perishing!"*
> *And he awoke and rebuked the wind and the raging waves, and they ceased,*
> *and there was a calm. He said to them, "Where is your faith?" And they were*
> *afraid, and they marveled, saying to one another, "Who then is this, that he*
> *commands even winds and water, and they obey him?" (Luke 8:23–25)*

1. What are the tangible things in your life for which you are grateful?

2. What storms in your life have tested your faith that God is close and in control?

3. What does God tell Tessa that personally brings you hope?

 TRUST

Close your eyes. Imagine yourself in a small boat, vulnerable, tossed by wind-whipped waves. The sky is dark. It is cold. What do you fear most? For you, what events/situations make your life like this storm? Picture yourself there, with everything out of control. What do you cling to? Ask Jesus to show you where he is, in the midst of it. What do you see him doing? What does he say? And now . . . how do you respond?

PRAY

Father, this heart of mine struggles to see you. I want to see you in the small things in my day. I confess to you my ingratitude, my hard heart that focuses on dangers more than the good of your promises. Help me to see you, desire to search for you and be a light shining with you, filled with faith to help others, in turn, see. In Jesus' name, Amen.

Small Groups and Scribbles

HE IS PULLING UP. I can hear the roll of the engine, the car door opening, the crunch of loafers on gravel walk. My chest tightens. Why can I barely breathe?

He's been encouraging me to get help, to talk to someone about this shame he thinks I carry around. He's been open with guys from church about his own issues, and when he comes home from work in the evenings, he is energized, loving, and supportive. It is so annoying.

I know that it's crazy, God, for me to think my husband, who loves me, is *annoying* me by suggesting, so gently, so delicately, "Maybe you shouldn't have to try to figure this all out on your own? I want to help you. There is something God is stirring in you. I wonder if you need to be healed?"

Be healed? *Grrr.* He says it like it is a prescription I can pick up at the pharmacy.

"Ask your doctor if Heal-O-Phanatic is right for you!"

I don't even want to know those side effects . . . probably'll turn me into a straight-up Stepford Wife.

I'm dodging now. But I will admit: I do think I'm hurting our kids with my negativity. I yell. A lot.

Chris left the door open to the car last night, and my battery was dead this morning, when I was already late to my meeting. I lost it in the driveway, in front of his friends, just as he was walking up the steps to our porch from school. His poor face was bright red.

I'm angry. So angry. Often. I haven't shared this with the ladies I'm getting to know at the mom's group at church. So many of them look like they just have it all together. I know this can't be true; they must struggle sometimes, like me. One nice mom whom I am getting to know better did share some pretty heavy stuff, which I so appreciate. It takes courage to be vulnerable—courage, I would like to point out to you, *which I don't have.* I want to feel less alone in this. But I can't imagine letting people know what really goes on inside my house, behind closed doors. They probably all do it too. And there's a reason we don't talk about this stuff. Right?

I'm trying, okay? I'M TRYING.

I'm trying to take care of *everybody*.

I'm trying to be a person others can be around.

I'm trying to cook a few decent meals a week.

I'm trying to keep a house together.

I'm trying to keep my job together, so we can keep our mortgage together, so we can keep our lives together.

I'm trying to follow you (and not doing a fine job of it, I'd add).

I'm trying. I'm trying. I'm trying.

It's not working.

God, is this my *life*?

LIFE IS A WHIRLWIND—it dizzies you.

But I am here, the eye of the winds, holding you fast. I am here in this boisterous kitchen as the hurricane circles in chaos—children and pots flying, torn recipe books, peelings and paychecks and shouts and laughs and howls and tears and try-try-trying. I am here, in the circle of women with whom you meet. I am here, in the conversations with Todd, in the upending of all the good things you thought you were. I catch you, each time you think you fall. You are held; I'll never let go.

Now cease trying. Bend your head, daughter. Let me heal you.

You shall be very low until I raise you up.

Healing is not fixing what is broken.

Healing is being transformed.

Healing is being restored to newness.

Healing is surrender.

Healing is *me*.

Listen for me. Trust—my wisdom will come, and all the fruits of it. Look for me. Trust—I am here. Believe my love. Trust—I am good.

Look, I restore all things.

 **LISTEN**

Elisabeth resists surrender. She tries to keep her life under her own control. Consider Elisabeth's questions to God. What is your prayer to him? Write it here.

THINK

> *Therefore, if anyone is in Christ, he is a new creation.*
> *The old has passed away; behold, the new has come. (2 Corinthians 5:17)*

1. Do you believe you're a mess? Have you ever tried to fix yourself, be less of a mess? How did it go?

2. How are you desperate for God's healing regarding wanting to be the one in control?

3. With what community can you see yourself taking a risk, sharing your heart, and asking for help regularly? What burden have you been carrying alone that God is inviting you to share with a friend?

 TRUST

Close your eyes. Consider how you feel when there are things you can't fix, can't control, can't change. How do you need God's healing? Ask God to reveal to you how he is inviting you to trust him. And then ask him with whom—with what friend in your life—you can share this. Wait for him. Listen. Ask him for courage to surrender all areas of your life to him, completely. And then share this act of surrender with a friend. Or do it with her. We are not made to walk this life alone.

PRAY

Father, I confess I want an easy answer, I want *my* answer. I confess I don't like to trust you. I confess I think the best way to live is to be the boss of my life, to have everything under my control. I struggle with surrendering my whole heart, my whole life, letting myself believe you care for me, you love me—that you care for all of us. Holy Spirit, come. Free me of this pride. I give it to you. Jesus, cleanse me. I surrender my heart. Father, I trust you are here, and you love me and will make me new. In your name, Amen.

*Look to me, child. Look at where I am,
in the midst of the hard things. Look to me
and how I am here, present with you. Look to me,
at my truth that I place in your heart. For I am
with you even when you can't see me. I am with
you even when your questions aren't answered.
I am with you, offering my presence
when all around you feels only night.*

Night Walking

THE STREETS ARE COLD TONIGHT.

Dirty sidewalk slick, gray. I'm going to slip, just watch. Go around the stuff Freddie didn't pick up from that shaggy mutt of his that does its thing *wherever*. Skirt piles of bottles. It's not pretty here. Garbage blown against the curbs, needles in wadded toilet paper, used Kotex and empty chip wrappers. Caroline's over there, huddled up under her fleece blanket. I forget who gave that to her. Oh yeah, she found it, she says. Yeah, resourceful, is what you call her. You have to be, out here.

You watching me walking out here, Lord? These nights when my big toes rub hard against the plastic of these old tennis shoes and my back seizes and my stomach aches. I'm hungry, yeah. But really, I'm *tired*. That everything-aches-kind-of-tired. It's cold.

There are days I know you're out here with me. And nights like this when I know you aren't anywhere close. Why would you be? I don't blame you for taking off. Probably not how you planned it to be, anyway, is it?

I get it. I thought leaving would be better than staying, too. Who could know the leaving would be the easiest part and that the staying out here will be what kills me, in the end? Funny, huh? Things don't go like we think.

God, I don't blame you for taking off. But you're a hypocrite.

I cough blood sometimes. Not sure how many more years, or months, or weeks I've got left. I feel better when I think maybe there won't be too many. Wherever you went has to be better than here. I don't want to be here, either.

I don't get how Momma sang "Jesus loves me" and told me how beautiful heaven is and how you'd always watch over me, no matter where I go. The truth is, I'm alone. Deep down, I always knew I would be. Dying alone, piled in trash. Alone, and you don't care. I'd love to believe, but you let life kill that plan.

God, it's dark. I'd love a burger. Nights like this must be what hell is like. Silent, the only choice whether to walk or freeze.

For now, I guess I'll walk.

Alone.

MY BABY GIRL, I'm sorry. My baby girl, I've got you, no matter how you feel. I am sorry you cannot see me. I am sorry you are cold and you have no food. I am sorry your feet hurt and you don't know if I care.

For I love you.

I stand over this city, mightier than armies. But I also walk these streets with you, curled into the small places. I look into the hearts of my children of vacancy. Even if you make your bed in the needle heap, I am there.

This is a waiting time. There is darkness in it. I will wipe it clean. I will wash the streets. I will wrap my arms around each daughter and son who lies as if dead. I see Caroline. I see Freddie. I see George and Briana. I see Pamela crying and confused, spitting at invisible things under the streetlamps. I see the children who have lost hope and are looking, simply, to survive.

I see you.

I want you to do more than survive, Renee. Because simply surviving is not living—although I want to help you survive first so that you can live. I care about the details of your life—whether you have food to eat and clothes to wear and a place to sleep. I care about the details of surviving, and I care about your living, too.

For every person out here on these streets—and the people not on these streets to whom I want to come and bring justice and love—I want to grab hold of their shoulders and look them in the eyes and ask them to awake! "Awake!" I want to shake their bodies, stir their hearts, and show them I am here. *I am here.*

Can you hear me? Can you hear my voice?

I am here in the night as much as in the day.

My anger burns against the evil on these streets where darkness covers and light does not shine. My anger burns for the daughters and sons I ask to come help and who don't. My anger burns against every denial of my presence on earth as it is in heaven. For there are many children, not just on these streets, who have known my name and denied me. And I love them, and there will be a day when I say, "I don't know you."

My heart sings over the children of the night. And here, on these streets, are the children of the day, too. I know you, Renee.

My daughter, my dear one. Call for me again. Heaven is where I am. Here. I am not far.

Awake.

 LISTEN

Picture Renee, walking the streets at night, cold and alone. She can't see past her circumstances, so she doubts God's closeness. What is your prayer, in response to Renee's conversation with God?

THINK

Yet he is actually not far from each one of us, for
"In him we live and move and have our being." (Acts 17: 27-28)

1. Renee struggles, walking the city streets in winter, homeless and cold and hungry, wondering if God is anywhere near. In what circumstances have you felt God is not with you?

2. God tells Renee he cares about the details of her life. How is it more or less difficult for you to believe God is with you in adversity?

3. Who are the children of the night and who are the children of the day? In what tangible way does God's anger prompt you to respond now?

 TRUST

Get in a quiet place. Think of a moment you have experienced adversity, struggle, or sought God's presence in need. Remember the sounds around you, what things looked like, smelled like, felt like, who was nearby. What was your heart's cry to God in that moment, when you felt desperate, when things were falling apart and you needed God to be there? Use your imagination and let yourself stay in that place for a while, remembering how you felt. Ask God to show you where he was.

Now ask God to show you a person who is struggling to know God's love for them, right now. How does that person feel? In what tangible, specific way do they need you to love them and offer them hope, in Jesus' name?

PRAY

Father, you are with me, in all places, in all things. Nothing separates me from your love. You meet me in any adversity I face. Help me see you when I need you most. Also, help me partner with you to bring your love and hope to people who need comfort, shelter, food, companionship, friendship, love. In Jesus' name, Amen.

In Beautiful Wild

THE KIDS ARE OUT IN THE YARD with the dog and the bunnies. I know they wish I would run out and play, too. Sunlight is pouring in through the windows, and I stand in it, arms at my side, eyes closed. If I squeeze my eyes tight enough, I can see the light shine on my eyelids, a dance of yellow and white and pink, a celebration of bursting light in shadowed dark.

Last night, Peter clasped my hand. We walked out the back door while the kids were sleeping. Driveway gravel crunched under our feet; it jarred the silence after the cicadas had quieted. We walked into black velvet night under twinkling stars, up to the park a half a mile from the house. We dropped hands, and I stretched right out onto that cool grass, my bare right arm resting against Peter's side. He lay next to me, our eyes looking up at heaven.

Up in those stars, I can find you. Take me up higher, will you? I listen to Peter's breathing next to me, and my too-fast beating heart slows.

Oh, Abba-Father, I don't want to be afraid anymore. Please come again—come again for me.

My counselor encourages me to be brave, but she lets me take baby steps. She doesn't push me too far. She knows how difficult it is for me to leave my house, be around anyone other than Peter or my kids. She knows how the world feels big, too big for me—that I can't find my way in it. Even to go to her office once a week, she knows, is a journey of trial and of faith. I trust this is part of the hard work that is worth it. I trust this is part of your plan for healing me.

You are all in, and I need you to be all in. I need you to fill all my broken places. For I am still so much afraid.

I am afraid to venture out. I am afraid to speak. You are my only safe place. Is that okay? Is it okay that I feel like the world around me moves too fast? Is it okay that I like to run away with you, and stay there with you, and that the loneliness in other places is over-whelming sometimes?

I know you bring healing, but I have to do some hard work—doing things that require bravery, and trust, and risk to make the healing stick. You remind me I am made for risk-taking—that nothing is risky with you.

I don't go to church anymore. Peter doesn't go either. I am not a problem that needs to be fixed; this is how they made me feel. I am taking the steps to you, and I might go back to church if you want me to. You protect my heart, and I trust you.

Yes, I believe you.

How can I trust you more, living this life you've given me, when I still just want to hide? Can I just hide with you?

You are the only one, other than Peter, who I know for sure won't hurt me. I am so grateful that I know you the way I do. My knowing you, in my heart and mind, will help me follow you to where you want me to go.

I know you rescue me, and I know you carry me. I know you know my heart breaks a bit, each day, in this earthly world. I know you know I need you to put it back together.

And, really, because I know you're here, I'm getting to be okay with that.

YOU ARE THE WOMAN who stands at the door wide open and isn't afraid to go through. You are the woman who holds up her arms, fingers stretched wide, and boldly asks to be loved, heart wild and beautiful.

You are not afraid, no matter what you think. You are wild and beautiful, my daughter. I love you.

I love your soft heart, your gentle trust in my healing. I love your tenderness toward others. You reach out with your hands wide open, and you *keep* them open. I know you think you don't. I know you think you huddle down, clasp those arms around you tight, and feel afraid to go out and take risks. But you do take risks, my dear.

You are not marked fearful. You are not marked timid. You are not marked careful or sad or meek. You are bold and beautiful in your love. You are boisterous and powerful in how you love with your whole heart. You don't hold back, my love, and people are drawn to that heart.

I know it's stressful. I know the world feels too big. But you cannot hide, my Annie. There are people who need to meet you, be encouraged by you. And there are people I have for you to meet. Keep writing and looking for me. Go to that mother's group when Laura invites you. Go to the store with Peter.

You know me, and you know my laugh, and you are filled with me. So can we go further and deeper? Can we go to new places together? And can you share it with those I bring?

Can you speak with my heart, and can you trust me? You are my delight, my strong heart, and I love you; I know you trust me. So let's go. You are safe when you are with me.

So stay. And let's go.

Let's go.

 LISTEN

Imagine yourself as AnneMarie, outside, at night, under the skies, talking to God. What part of her prayer resonates with you the most? Where do you see yourself in this scene? Write your prayer to God in response.

THINK

There is no fear in love, but perfect love casts out fear.
For fear has to do with punishment, and whoever
fears has not been perfected in love. (1 John 4:18)

1. In what way have you ever felt a strong need to hide (emotionally, socially)? From whom or from what do you hide now?

2. In what way do you feel overwhelmed by the expectations of this world? How do you feel like you aren't enough, or that you don't fit in?

3. In his response to AnneMarie, what did you most need to hear God say?

 TRUST

Go to a quiet place. Close your eyes. Let God show you how he looks at you. Let him reveal how he laughs with joy because of you. Stay here. Wait on him. Trust he loves you. Trust he wants to be with you and reveal to you how much he enjoys being with you, his beloved, his daughter.

PRAY

Father, this world intimidates, with its fast pace and endless demands. I can easily believe I'm not brave enough, strong enough, intelligent enough. I confess the pressure I feel makes me want to hide. I surrender to you all my fears. Help me be present with you, accepting your love for me and the beautiful way I was made by you. Give me courage to go where you lead me. With you, I have no fear. In Jesus' name, Amen.

Slammed Doors and Open Windows

THE DOOR TO HIS BEDROOM IS CLOSED, slammed so hard it lodged shut. We argued again last night, not about anything serious. But still my voice is a siren of exasperation at another response of "I don't know" and "chill out." And this morning, I got upset again when he staggered out to breakfast so late and almost missed the bus to school.

It used to feel like he was mine. I remember his small hands, dimpled and soft, reaching for me. I remember the sound of his voice, the call of "Mama" in the little cottage with the yellow walls. I remember light shining golden through the windows and him sitting on the floor with a basket of books, turning the stiff cardboard pages, then pushing his trucks around the room.

That's where he learned to scoot forward, his bottom in the air, his knees pressed into the wool carpet. He pulled his body forward with determination and the strength in his little shoulders and arms. He loved to move. And I would watch him and cheer him on. And then I would scoop him up and breathe in his pink cheeks and feel the softness of his hair against my skin. I miss him, Father.

I look back at those days when he was little, and I wonder if I appreciated them then. I wonder if I knew, in the rush of a day, how fleeting they would be. The days didn't feel short, but stretched long. Going to the grocery store was a full-on event that required preparation. I needed supplies: Cheerios in a plastic container with a lid and the blue padded fabric seat that wrapped around the metal shopping cart. This way, he could sit there, be busy with a snack, and not get germs on his eager little hands.

The days were divided into little pockets of time. Morning was breakfast, playtime, morning nap, snack, errands, a trip to the park. Afternoon was lunch and afternoon nap, playing, reading, going on walks to see friends, making dinner, bathtime, then stories and snuggles before bed. He was the child I loved to hold, the one I didn't want to put down. And now here I am, romanticizing a past and struggling to enjoy these present teenage moments, this present that feels so foreign, so removed from what once was.

I read all the parenting books on teenagers telling me this is normal, that his pulling away from me is good. I continue to hug him when he lets me, his body stiff and awkward, bending at the waist and leaning in just a little, shoulders bent forward, his fingers touching the back of my shoulders like I am a cactus, or a flower that needs to be handled with care. It bugs me, his posture, but I grab him firm anyway. *You can tell me anything, you know.* I pursue him in the quiet moments. The car rides to basketball practice, the minutes right at bedtime when I don't want to talk at all because I am tired but he is not. I pray, God, he will be open with me, turning to me with his questions, his worries and mistakes when he needs someone the most. Drugs, sex, parties, social media, pornography. Connection is more than communication and respect. I want to love him well, God, even when it is hard.

I want him to be independent, confident, resilient, resourceful, and kind. I want him to know he is loved, no matter what. Know that failure is okay. My prayer since he was born: that he would love you with all his heart, soul, mind, and strength. But here's the truth I don't want to admit: I've parented doubting that you have a better plan for him than I ever could have. I've parented believing his success, whether in loving you or in experiencing any achievement—in school, in sports, in career—is up to me. I confess I've lived trusting my parenting more than yours.

And I repent. I don't want to do that anymore.

Oh God. I give him back to you . . .

. . . AND I RECEIVE HIM. I remember those early days, daughter. I remember when you weren't sure how to mother. You stumbled into it with confidence, with love, with patience. You knew how to love him, that boy of yours, and you gave him all of you. You never asked for anything back. You can do that again.

Don't doubt, despite all these trials, that you are beautiful to me, child.

But he did give you so much, didn't he? In the moments of outstretched hands, of giggles and cries. He needed you, and it feels so good to be needed, to be wanted, desired. But know this: Even in the pushing away that he is doing now, he is still crying out; he is still reaching; he is wondering if you are still here, his safety, his sure one. He needs you, his mom, dear one, even though it doesn't feel like it sometimes.

And you've needed me too.

I know it is hard to not look back on the past. It is good to remember the beauty of moments, the preciousness of memory. You carry those stories within you, child. You carry the memory within you; it has shaped you, and reminds you that it's okay to not have this life all figured out. Now you know you are not alone. Now you see me here with you. I am holding your boy as I hold you, my arms wrapped fast around you both. Especially now.

You are not alone. Not then, when he was small and the smiles came readily and easily. And not now, with his reticence to give of himself. I will help him take risks. I will be with him as he tries new things. Yes, I know that this world feels so much bigger and more dangerous than ever before. He'll be okay. Even when it feels like he won't. I am here. I hear your prayers. I keep my arms wrapped 'round.

Look to me. How you feel and what you know are not what I feel and what I know. I see you. I see your darling boy. There is a future here that is good. Yes, even in this journey now. Yes, even though it is hard.

Yes, I take your fear. Yes, I take your worry. I've had him all along. You too.

And this is still just the beginning.

 LISTEN

Bree wants to surrender the parenting of her teenage son to God. What emotions do you feel when you hear Bree's and God's conversation? What is your prayer to God in response?

 THINK

He will not let your foot be moved; he who keeps you will not slumber.
Behold, he who keeps Israel will neither slumber nor sleep.
The LORD is your keeper; the LORD is your shade on your right hand.
The sun shall not strike you by day, nor the moon by night.
The LORD will keep you from all evil;
he will keep your life.... (Psalm 121:3-7)

1. You don't need to be a parent to struggle to connect with someone after a relationship has changed in some way. What relationship are you struggling with now? What, in the response Bree hears from God, offers you comfort?

2. How easily do you accept this response to Bree: "It's okay to not have this life all figured out"? What fear is God prompting you to give to him?

3. Reread the prayer you wrote. What else do you want to say to God?

 TRUST

Be quiet for a few moments. Consider what you struggle surrendering to God, what you wish you could change–a person or a situation or a condition you wish could be fixed. Close your eyes and picture the person or situation. See it clearly. Then ask God to help you let it go. Open your hands, let them fall at your side or rest in your lap. Give God this thing you've been holding onto. Trust him with your mind, your heart, your imagination now. Let him show you a new picture of what it means to have your hands open, giving this person or situation to him.

PRAY

Father, change is hard. I resist it. I fight when I see it coming. I want to control the details of my life, to manage the people I love and make sure they're okay. Uncertainty undermines my faith. Forgive me. I surrender to you the people I love most, and I pray that I may be the woman who loves my family and friends well. I surrender all my roles to you. I pray that you are seen in me, more than anything else. I want to trust you more than myself. In Jesus' name, Amen.

Cool and Beautiful

I FLIP THROUGH THE PAGES of the catalogue. The girl on the cover looks cute, her brown hair flowing down past her shoulders and her blunt, straight bangs. She grips an "I got you Babe" coffee cup with a big red heart on the front. She smiles down at a stout bulldog with droopy cheeks and pink, wet tongue and has the word "Marlowe" written on her arm in black marker. So cool. I study her outfit, her hairstyle, her expression, and wonder if I could pull this look off, too.

Doubtful.

She appears indifferent to the camera, happy in the moment, confident to be who she is.

Hmm, does she really have it together? It sure looks good from here.

Good grief.

Yeah, I know this is an ad for young women's clothing. I know it's not real. But, maybe? *Get a grip, girl.* Okay. It's official. I'm obsessed. *Stop looking.* She just looks so cool. I want to be her.

Yeah, I know, God—she is just an image, a photograph, an airbrushed-like-crazy fake-girl-model advertising the cool, hip lifestyle the clothing company is trying to sell. Yeah, I know I won't be more content if I suddenly won the lottery and my fairy godmother gave me a closet full of awesome, cool clothes.

Ugh. But I would feel better about myself, I think. Yeah, for sure I would.

Right?

Well, I am *so* not her. I can't even fake it.

It's not that her skin is light and mine isn't. It's not that I don't have a budget right now to buy designer clothes or makeup—or the imagination or creativity to fill my Instagram feed with images that make me look put-together-casual-awesome. Nope. No hipness here, if that's a word.

I study her more.

Her appearance is actually a bit of a mess; her hair is disheveled, her jeans are torn. Crumpled papers litter the desk where she sits. Huh. Because the thing is, God, she clearly does not give a care about the disarray she is sitting right down in the middle of one bit. She just sits there, gazing at her drooling bulldog and smiling. *I am young and beautiful and don't care about my messy desk or my drooling dog (isn't he adorable?) because I just look so beautiful and cool, don't I?*

I can hear you say it, God, telling me the opposite of what I believe is true. That I'm perfectly beautiful, that I'm perfectly designed. But, and I hate to tell you this, but here it is: These sweet things you say sometimes feel like just . . . *words*. I struggle to believe you. Okay, I admit; it feels kind of crazy-awesome, actually, to imagine that, in my mess, despite all of my mistakes and wounds and wishes-I-were-different, you are here loving me—even smiling probably—sticking close, wanting me to believe that not only do you love me . . . you actually like me, too.

You. Are. Crazy.

I like it.

Do you remember what happened last week?

My friend asks me to come over. We go to her room and she plays a song that is just so *her* . . . so *you*. A voice sings soft, then grows louder. The musician sings as if she is listening to your voice. She sings as if she is telling me something right from you: "I am not surprised by who you are. I am not disappointed by how you look, how you are made. I knew what was coming when I made you. You are broken, and I am with you. I am not shocked or sad or disappointed or having second thoughts about you. I love you, you know that. And I like you. I like you, too."

I guess I didn't know I needed to hear that. Yeah, God, you're right; I get that you love me—that's the kind of God you are. But to hear that you *like* me? Even though I'm not the most beautiful girl, not the most cool and hip? Even though I'm a mess—and not the cool kind of mess like in the magazine, but the *not-cool* kind of mess—with a body I wish were smaller, hair I wish were tamer, teeth I wish were whiter, a voice I wish was wittier, a mind I wish was smarter.

Yeah?

Will I truly feel joy and freedom, God, when I accept I'm okay, like this? How do I get there, and when?

I LOVE YOU, you know that? I get that you are wondering how this love I have for you can penetrate—can get from head to heart. That is what is most important. That is how you carry with you weapons that fight the lies—the ones that tell you beauty looks like this, and not like that. Listen close. Because who can decide what is beautiful better than me, the one who created beauty to begin with? I only create what is beautiful, you know.

And there it is. It might be as simple as that, knowing I create only beauty, and I created you. But now, I know it doesn't feel that simple. Not at all. I know that the lies of this world complicate things a lot. I know you are distracted. You see a young woman and you can't help but compare yourself to her. You see a photograph in a magazine, a mannequin in a storefront, the images on your phone. You see her face, watch how she walks, listen to her jokes, count how many friends and followers she has. And where does that get you? This isn't truth, and this isn't full life, and this isn't how you will ever be joy-filled and free.

That's what I've planned for you: joy, strength, confidence, freedom. Protect your heart now, Bella. You've got to give your heart to me. That is the choice you have, the action you need to take for your heart to be protected: surrender. You need to surrender your heart to me.

These aren't just words for you to contemplate. It is time for you to act. Look at your face in the mirror, for starters. Look at those eyes, the shape, the lashes, the way you blink. Look at your cheekbones, how exquisite and perfect. Look at your lips, how vulnerable and strong they are. Your hands, your neck, your feet, your stomach, your legs, your knees, your skin. Each part of you I put together with my own breath, my love. I chose the color of your skin, your hair, your lips, your eyes, your hands. I breathed life into you. I thought you up and made you, just like this. You can add adornment to beauty, but the adornment is not what shines. Be careful that adornment is not distraction from the beauty I create. And that is why I ask you to let me protect your heart.

Beauty is more than what you can see with your eyes—and I know you feel this tension. It's the beauty of the heart—true beauty—you're after, but you are tricked to believe beauty is something else. You feel the tension between the mirage—the attempt of the world to make beauty something that can be attained through a purchase of clothes, jewelry, technology—and the truth. It takes knowing me to recognize true beauty—to see it in others, to see it in yourself.

It's the heart, Bella. That's where true beauty lives. It takes faith in me to struggle with the tension of this world and my truth. It takes my strength in you to be confident in how I've made you, beautiful and loving and good. Daughter, true beauty is a heart that loves me. True beauty is sacrifice and surrender and worship—love—in my name.

You tell me how wonderful it is to hear that, not only do I love you, not only do I know you are beautiful, but that I also like you! My daughter, I adore you! I like you and love you and you know that. Your hearts knows that, Bella. So now surrender. Be free. Be beautiful. Be bold. Be fiery and fierce and alive, filled with my joy and love for you.

This is a battle to believe you are beautiful, after all. And you are equipped for this battle—the one where truth battles the lies of this world. Let me protect your heart. Let me deafen the lies.

There, now you see it, hear it, feel it.

Beauty.

Live believing you are beautiful.

Forget "coolness." This is how beauty sees.

 LISTEN

Bella is aware of the world's influences—defining for her what is beautiful and is not—yet she struggles to accept herself as she is. God speaks to her about true beauty. What do you think about her prayer with God and what he says back? Write your own prayer to God in response.

THINK

> *But the LORD said to Samuel, "Do not look on his appearance*
> *or on the height of his stature, because I have rejected him.*
> *For the LORD sees not as man sees: man looks on the outward*
> *appearance, but the LORD looks on the heart." (1 Samuel 16:7)*

1. How do you struggle with believing you are beautiful? What is the body part you dislike the most? Ask God what he sees when he looks at you. Ask him to show you not just how he sees your physical appearance, but also how he sees your heart.

2. How do you struggle with comparison or envy? How is God asking you to confess and ask for his help?

3. What agreements do you need to break with the enemy about your definition of beauty? List them. Break them now.

   > *Father, I break the agreement that . . .*
   > *I take it to the foot of the cross.*
   > *Fill me with your truth.*

4. Do you believe God likes you? What, specifically, does he like? Be bold. Be brave. Don't hold back. Spend a few minutes and write it all down . . . Then write some more.

TRUST

Find your Bible and a journal. Find a quiet place. Look up in your Bible the verses listed below about beauty. Pick one of the verses and practice Lectio Divina: (1) Read the verse several times or linger on one particular phrase or even one word. Don't rush. Ask God to reveal to you what it is in this verse–a word, an idea, an image–that he wants you to notice or pay attention to. (2) Meditate on what stood out to you. Imagine yourself in this verse. Place yourself as a character; try to see yourself, with Jesus, in this scene. (3) Respond, in prayer, to what God is showing you. (4) Give this time back to God. Surrender your heart to him and consider how you will live out what he has shown you.

1 Samuel 16:7	Galatians 3:26–27
Psalm 139:14	1 Timothy 4:8
Proverbs 31:30	1 Peter 3:3–5
Acts 10:34	

PRAY

Lord, you are the creator of all beauty, and I confess I get distracted with what the world defines as beauty. I chase that kind of beauty more than the beauty you create and see. And I love that you see beauty in me. I want to believe in that more, God. Help me to learn more about what beauty is to you. I want to live out the beauty you see in me. Silence the lies of the enemy that whisper I am not beautiful, I am not special, desired, liked, adored. In your name, Jesus, I break the agreement that beauty is what is defined by this world rather than what you see. You fill me with strength and light and hope. Thank you that you are here and you give the eyes of my heart a new way to see. In Jesus' name, Amen.

Mountainscapes and Heavensong

THE AIR IS SWEET HERE, summertime perfume. It blankets the meadow beyond the trees. My boots crunch gravel. I bend down, adjust my socks. There's a long way to go, a day's hike to the river before nightfall. This is going to be tough, isn't it? Yeah, but it will be awesome, too.

What were you thinking, God, when you painted the grass this green? Did you smile when you thought how shadows would move like dancers under the trees? Color bursts everywhere—I imagine you whispering death to life, your words speaking blue and green and brown. This flower stem you crafted with your hands. This wind on my cheek, your very breath. You are sweet, God. You are precious and lovely and amazing in how you love.

I think as I walk the trail, moving through this painting you created. This walking is dancing through it. You tell me I am an even more beautiful work of your love. I am your love dancing now—dancing in this canvas of beautiful brilliance.

You capture me with your love. You capture me with your

energy that flows through me, giving me this day to see and hear and feel you in my heart and on my skin and in my mind.

With you, I am your girl, your darling one. I am strong and free of all insecurities, all fear. I am rescued again. I recognize your song in my heart.

You are my delight. You carry me. You release me from the worry, the ache of an unknown future. There are times in life I feel like I can see the whole trail. Then there are times like this—where I can't even see much past the end of the day, and worry is always a few steps behind.

I wish I knew what was going to happen. Walking without answers is hard. All I can do is cling to you, my security, my safe and strong place. You will walk with me, won't you? I can go with you—and you with me—wherever you lead? Will you lead me where I can see you so I know where my feet need to tread? Will you stay where I can see you, where I can hear you? Will you be close when I don't know which way to turn?

I try to be strong, like you say I am, with you. I try to give you my fears—you say your love wipes them away. I try to believe it is in my weakness that I am strong, for then I can see you and rely on your strength in my life. And I keep walking, and I keep listening, and I just want to *be* with you, all the time.

Is that okay? Can we run now, through this meadow and down this hill? Can we jump and yell loud and tumble down into the flowers and let the sunlight shine on my eyelids closed tight? May I sing so that you think it is lovely? May I dance so you think it is beautiful? May I speak words of hope that show people you are in me and we are your light?

You are the lovely one, my King. You are the song, the dance, the rhythm of the orchestra of heaven. I want to be there, now, each day, each moment, with you.

It is not with earthly eyes that I see. Let me walk with you now, this heavensong singing high and strong and loud as the path stretches out. I cannot see what is next.

But I can see you.

I AM BURSTING WITH JOY for you. You are my precious one, and yes, we may dance, and yes, we may sing and yell and tumble down the meadow there. We can do it again and again.

Did you see those butterflies? What do you think about the strength of their bodies and the delicacy of their wings? They fly, my love. Oh, how they fly. When I look at you, I think of the butterflies— how they sing through the way they move, how stunning their colors are, how they land with such care and precision upon a stem, a bud, a branch.

Fly with me, my darling one. Let us fly and dance and be beauty in a world that is blind to it. You see more than what can be seen. You hear more than what can be heard. You feel more than what can be touched. For you claim me in you—and with me, you begin to see heaven. With me, you can fly. With me, you can go where you could never go on your own. Your strength is not what can be seen. Your hope is not what can be measured.

You are yourself and not yourself. You are becoming what I have always seen. Come now, my darling one, farther under my wings. Know the feel of my heart against your skin. When we fly you will have courage to go into the unknown, for I will be with you wherever I ask you to go. There are places you get to go now, now that you see me and you hear me and you love me and you seek me with your whole heart.

It is deeper into the folds and out into the shadows, and where light does not touch the ground where I need my light in you to shine.

So, yes, sing my love, for I give you songs to sing. Yes, dance my love, for I give you steps in sync with mine. Yes, reach out and wrap your arms around the people to whom I draw you close. You are light and love and hope—my light shining so brightly in you, my darling one.

Let us go. Higher still, and farther. Into the places you have yet to see and hear and feel.

I will smile on you. I do smile on you.

I will show you—there is so much more to come.

 LISTEN

Imagine Holly hiking. Consider her posture with God, how she delights in him and feels free to express to him her fear of the unknown. What is your reaction to their conversation? Write your own prayer here.

 THINK

As the Father has loved me, so have I loved you.
Abide in my love. (John 15:9)

1. Imagine Holly walking with you. What would you ask her?

2. In God's response to Holly, what does he say that captured your imagination, encouraged you, or made you wonder about God?

3. How do you understand what God says to Holly: "You are yourself and not yourself. You are becoming what I have always seen"?

 TRUST

If you can, go for a walk in the fresh air. If you can't, imagine it. Find a place where you can be free and uninhibited. Close your eyes, lift your arms out, tilt your head back. Or represent, with your body, whatever posture it is you feel symbolizes your whole self—your head, heart, and soul—being fully present to God. Imagine what it means for you to be "all in" with God—even if the future is unknown. Ask God to take control of your direction.

PRAY

Jesus, remove my hesitation to be present with you. Let me *want* to experience your closeness; let me *want* to experience worshipping you without reservation. Let me come into your presence and receive your grace—your Spirit filling me with your joy, hope, and peace. Let me walk with you in this sacred space, no matter where I am or where I am going. Help me worship you in all situations, in all places. Let me fall more deeply in love with you. In your name I pray, Amen.

My lovely one, close your eyes now.
For I am here, in the long days. I am here,
in the uncertainty. I am here, in the exhaustion.
I am here, in the wondering of what's next
and when and how.

Eulogy at the Kitchen Sink

I STAND AT THE KITCHEN SINK, dipping my hands into the water. It's still warm. Suds reach my wrist, and I retrieve the plate crusted with marinara from last night's dinner. I force white to glisten beneath smears of red and brown.

There was a book I read that made doing the dishes sound beautiful, miraculous even. She could stand at the kitchen sink, and the sparkle of dish soap would help her see heaven. Heaven feels far away from me. I don't feel like one of the beautiful ones—or one who could find beauty here.

The water is murky now. Bits of grease float up to the surface. Iridescent orbs of color. Bubbly suds form a thin white crust in one corner of the sink. I can't see my hands.

I pull out the last grease-crusted plate. Why doesn't light flood through my window, making these soap bubbles dance and shine?

It's quiet here, the silence a noose around my neck.

Once, the noise was loud—the voices raised, the tension high. She would get so angry, and I would get angry, too, and yell back, even louder. I didn't like it. But I don't like this silence any better.

I miss her, not the way her shoes piled up by the door or how she kept her room—so I couldn't even stand to have the door open. But I miss her face, the feel of her skin under my hand. I miss tucking her dark curls behind her ears.

And when I kissed her, when she was little, she smelled of apple oatmeal and vanilla soap. My heart aches for her now.

On days like these, on so many days, the silence feels too much for me. I am all alone now; she has moved so far. My heart can't bear to keep *remembering* her. And yet I fear *forgetting* even more.

Oh, God, how many more days must I stand here, remembering, dipping tired hands into now cold dishwater in this old kitchen sink? I ache for the silence to lift, for her loss to fade.

Reading your words in my Bible isn't working. Honestly, I can scarcely read a page I get so tired, the days I rise and leave my bed. The doctor urges me to take the medication so the darkness feels less severe. But I don't have faith in light shining soon.

I guess this is how it will be in twenty years or so, short and simple. Not much to say:

Diane Lindsey, age seventy-something, passed away peacefully (I hope) after a battle with clinical depression. Diane was a loving daughter, mother, wife, and active member of the church.

Born to Louis and Elaine Matthews in Moreland Hills, she lived in Upper Arlington and retired from the Upper Arlington library after twenty-seven (or so) years.

She is survived by her husband, Frank, and daughter, Jessica (whom she loved).

The end.

Somehow, my legs keep holding me. And I lift my hands and plunge them down once more into murky water. Here, a gleaming porcelain plate.

ONE ARM UP NOW, DARLING. And then the other. Let me take off these bindings. They are heavy and not for you. No, you are not meant to wear this shroud.

You are light and carefree, and you need to give me the bindings now. I lift them off of you. One remnant of cloth and then the next—invisible and strong so you can scarcely move.

You are made to move with me, my love. I sing to you a song your heart knows, for you are not forgotten. I see you. I see your beauty. I behold you, and I behold your light, and I remove the shrouds so your light can freely shine.

I know these grave clothes are what you feel you've always worn, at least for too many years. You can't remember not worrying, not wondering how to love her so she would love you the way you needed to be loved.

But you never told her how much you loved her, and you scarcely let me love you. And now the grave clothes are too heavy, and the gravestone is marked, etched with a testimony I did not write for you.

May I share with you the testimony, the eulogy, I want to write on your heart, a place that is not a grave at all but a light that shines?

This darling one shines brighter than any star I have cast into the heavenly sky. She is more beautiful than a teardrop on her daughter's cheek, more delicate and strong than the stem of a single rose. I have carried her, and she sees my arms around her when her arms are lifted high.

She lifts them high, and her shroud is gone. Her new clothes are white, and light shines through the garments that flow down from her outstretched arms. They sing, this light.

Her life is music now, and she keeps hands up, fingers out-stretched, for she knows what freedom is, how light dances from her as she walks, each step one of beauty, a painting too beautiful and yet completely true.

For she is awake now. She is alive now. Each step now with her king.

I see this, child. Come now. Enter in. What I see is the truest. What I speak is the music your heart needs to hear. Come now. You are free. Shrouds are long gone.

 LISTEN

Sit in the quiet for a few moments—five minutes, if you can. Consider Diane's heart cry to God and his response. What is your prayer?

THINK

Fear not, for I am with you; be not dismayed,
for I am your God; I will strengthen you, I will help you,
I will uphold you with my righteous right hand. (Isaiah 41:10)

1. What will you remember about Diane? How does she struggle? What are her fears? What are your fears?

2. When can you relate to feeling sad, lonely, and alone? What is God asking you to give to him?

3. In God's response to Diane, what did you, also, need to hear God say?

 TRUST

Be bold now. Get out some paper. Sit in a comfy chair. Write your eulogy. Fill a page or two with a description of who you were, how you spent your life, how people remember you, what they loved about you. Write it the way God would, through the lens by which he sees you. You're pretty awesome, after all. For real. He's going to make sure that important fact is communicated. How does God see you?

PRAY

Father, let your light in. Shine bright on me, on my fears, my heart, my life. I want to see with clear eyes what you see. I want to see your goodness, all the possibilities I can struggle to believe are real, or are for me. You see beauty where there is brokenness. You see light where there is darkness. You see hope where there is despair. I surrender to you my insecurities. One by one . . . here they are . . . (name them). I give you my mind, my heart, my soul. Let me live in the confidence of who I am, the truth of me, only what you see. I claim only what you see. In Jesus' name, Amen.

Fall

IN EVERY SPACE OF THE HOUSE I made sure I could see her face. Photos taped to the fridge, matted in fancy silver frames on the bookshelf, propped next to the plants on the table by my bed. I thought having her smile everywhere would make her feel closer. But it didn't. I grabbed each one today and pushed them into an old file box and put them in the garage.

She was sick my teenage years, on the couch for hours at a time. I would tiptoe through the living room as she slept, missing the mom who laughed and planned, the mom who loved and filled a room with life.

I decided, when the diagnosis came, that I needed to do whatever I could to make her better. Be *quiet* when she was sleeping. Come *right* home after school. Get *good* grades. Don't go to *parties*. Don't get involved in *sports*. Keep my room *clean*. Be *present*. Be *available*. *Don't* make her worry. Be a good girl, and *get everything right*.

I loved her, God.

I loved her, and I wanted her to stay. She never complained. She never asked me to be perfect. I loved her, and I didn't know what to do to help her. So I made a decision: try to be the best daughter I could. Did it even do any good? It didn't help her stay.

I ache inside, God. I ache for her smile. I ache for her voice. I ache for her laugh, the laugh that would fill me up and make me feel safe and let me know, without a doubt, I was home.

With her, wherever I was, I was home.

My mom's illness and death have made me strong. But not the kind of strong that accepts weakness in myself. Her death makes me afraid, I think. I am afraid to be weak. If I'm weak, the people I love will surely fall.

That's the problem. My head knows you are probably the safe place, the strong one—not me. But my heart doesn't believe it. (This prayer right now is risky, and I'm afraid to say it.) God, help. I am hurting, sad, alone—but mostly, I'm so tired of believing the lie that being strong means holding together what is not mine to hold.

God, please hear me: Really, I am so afraid to let go and fall.

MY DAUGHTER, TAKE OFF YOUR SHOES. Come with me. Let me show you a place that is holy.

When I made you, you were crafted to look like me. You have within you my breath. My words breathed on you and in you. And what I see when I look on you, what I see when I stand with you, my shining one, is what is holy. You are pure and you are untarnished. You are shining now. You are glorious now. You are filled with light now. My daughter, I've never let you go.

I filled the room when I cared for your mother and I cared for you. I filled the rooms of your home, walked with you at school, guarded you while you slept. You are precious to me, and I know it was so hard when she was sick. I know how you were scared and you didn't want her to worry. I know how you tried to be strong and do the right thing.

Do you know I am so proud of you? Do you know I stay with you, and I watch you, and I fill you with me because I love you? Do you know I have even more of me to give you? Do you know I have amazing things to show you?

Now hear this: It is not because you weren't strong enough that your mom died. It is not because you did or didn't do the right thing. I am the one who carried your mom. I am the one who protected her heart. I am the one who guarded her, and stayed with her, and filled her with peace. That joy she had? That love she had for you? It was because she knew me. It was because she trusted me. Do you want to know me more? Do you want to trust me?

You carry within you her inheritance, the blessing of being known, the blessing of being loved, the blessing of being protected and filled with joy.

You are my joy-carrier, my darling. I fill you with my joy. Carry it on; carry it forward. It is me you are carrying. It is me you are beholding. It is me you are showing to those you love. Just point to me, living out freedom, not bondage. Living out joy, not striving to keep it all together.

So this is what you're going to have to do: You're going to have to break the agreement with the evil one that you are weak when you are not strong. You have to break the agreement that I can't be counted on to be strong for you when you need me most. You need to break the agreement that weakness is dangerous, risky—that you need only work harder to be protected, to prevent tragedy, to be strong.

You have to surrender these lies to me and let me replace them with my truth: My Son came and took all of your sin, and in him you are given grace and you are redeemed and you have the Holy Spirit in you to equip you to do anything I have for you to do in my name. Try it. Break the agreements. Let me fill you with truth and love. Ask me to come. Ask me again to help you fall and be free and soar.

Remember, I am the one who holds you together. Letting yourself go is the only way to carry forth that joy in you.

You can't try harder now, love. Fall into my arms, and I'll catch you.

I promise.

In falling, you will fly.

 **LISTEN**

Clementine suffers from believing the lie that God can't be counted on, that *she* is the one who needs to be strong. How do you see yourself in Clementine? What emotions do you feel? What do you want to say to God in response?

THINK

> *But he said to me, "My grace is sufficient for you,*
> *for my power is made perfect in weakness."*
> *Therefore I will boast all the more gladly of my weaknesses,*
> *so that the power of Christ may rest upon me. (2 Corinthians 12:9)*

1. How have you tried to be strong, the one who does the right thing for the sake of another? What are the consequences of trying to be perfect when you can't be?

2. How do you let yourself be okay with being weak, trusting that God is the one who is strong?

3. What, if anything, is difficult for you to believe in what God says to Clementine?

4. Sometimes we live as if we've made agreements with the darkness to allow it into our lives. What agreements with the enemy do you need to break? What have you believed about God, or about yourself, that just aren't true scripturally? Name the lies–name what you have been believing and ask God to replace them with his truth. Break those agreements now. (God, I break the agreement that . . .)

 TRUST

Get out a piece of paper. Find a pen that works. Write at the top of the paper, "Dear . . ." and write your name. Then write, "I am so proud of you . . ." Now, without censoring yourself, write down five, ten, or twenty things that demonstrate how you are perfectly made, even in your weakness. Sign the letter: Love, God.

PRAY

Father, you are the strong one. You delight in me, in my weakness. You love me just as I am. I confess I try to hold things together, that I try to be perfect, and that I struggle feeling okay when I fail. I give you the moments when I first began to believe the lie that I am not good enough, and that I need to be perfect to be loved. Bring more healing to my heart. Bring more surrender. I give you my desire to be strong and in control. You have me. Let me live a life believing that. In Jesus' name, Amen.

EMILY

Morning in the Studio

JUST BARE FEET TODAY, NO one here. Too early. The rehearsal schedule, a long paper rectangle smudged with ink, is taped to the wall. I don't want to look at it. Can't today hold a moment where I dance by myself, with no one around? Yet I've forgotten how.

I used to dance with abandon, before dancing became a job. Now it's almost a chore. Do you remember, years ago? I didn't know the names of any positions or movements. "Choreography" was a word other people used. Dance, then, was how I told stories. It was the two of us. This music? These were our songs.

How did I lose my love for the thing I loved most? Joy feels so elusive now. I obsess over what I look like when I dance—whether I am beautiful, perfect, flawless in form. I mean, how do I doubt doing what I once used to love?

I used to dance alone in a room and know what I did was beautiful—something I knew I was made to do. As a little girl, how could I *not* dance when the light streamed in through my window each morning? How could I *not* pull on the pink tulle dress that dragged in the back, the one Mom still let me wear even after the sequins no longer sparkled and shined? How could I *not* use the sidewalk like a dance studio on my way to school, or respond to the music I heard you sing to me, so lovingly, so tenderly, in my heart?

I heard you, even though I didn't know then it was you. I love how you did that, God. I have missed dancing with you.

I have lost my way. Maybe I don't know what I love to do anymore. Perhaps it is because I feel all eyes are on me, judging whether what I do is good enough or not. When did that lie come in, God—the lie that I am not enough? If I know what you've made me to do with you, how do I do it? How do I claim it? How do I silence fear, remember what is true about how you've made me, step out, and just go?

YES, YOU KNOW these steps, this song. I've taught you each move. Now speak the lyrics to me. Let's translate this music I've given your heart.

First, be bold in trusting the talents I've given you, how I've made you to love other people, to bring joy and hope to this world. To do this, you must stay with me. Respond to the rhythm I set, each step. Embrace how you're uniquely made to live. Stand and do what I've gifted you to be able to do.

When you do this, I have more for you. I conquer fear in you, so you can trust me when there is a new move, a new step. You love to dance, but it is not just dancing now, is it? Doing what you're made to do represents freedom, joy, and hope. I know you want to say yes to what I have written on your heart.

I have freedom for you—rejecting a life of anxiety or fear of regret. Keep your eyes on me; you can see me. With me, you can do the things you are made to do.

I have joy for you—living in my love for you while pursuing the passions I've given you. Joy is a surrendered heart that leads and loves. I shine light, you know, in the dark.

I have hope for you—living all-out for the future that is to come. It is knowing heaven is here, within you, for I am in you. Hope is knowing there is no separation between us, so you are unafraid to take risks. You see heaven in your heart and you want more. You know I'm coming, daughter.

Emily, this is the life I've given you. No other. Come on now. Look to me. Listen to your heart. Take the steps I put in front of you. Go beyond where you know I am but you can't see. Yes, this is dancing. And so much more.

Go, daughter. I am with you!

Dance!

Leap!

Love!

Bend!

Know!

Be!

Become!

Sway!

Bow!

Go!

 LISTEN

Emily seeks freedom and joy in dancing—in doing what God has made her to do with him. What resonated with you most when you listened to this conversation between Emily and her Father? What prayer do you want to speak to him now? Write it here.

THINK

Behold, you are beautiful, my love, behold, you are beautiful!
Your eyes are doves behind your veil. Your hair is like a flock of goats
leaping down the slopes of Gilead. (Song of Solomon 4:1)

1. Name one or two activities you love to do, things that make you feel most alive.

2. What gets in the way of you doing these activities regularly? What prevents you from feeling awake and beautiful and free?

3. What "dancing" is God calling you to do with him, right now?

 TRUST

Think of a piece of artwork you love—a painting hanging in your house or found on the Internet. Or think of your very favorite color, the color that you feel best represents you—your beauty, your heart, the things you most love to do. Now close your eyes. Imagine yourself, first, in an empty white space . . . and then imagine the painting or the color comes down behind you, like a backdrop in the scene of a play.

See yourself walking into that painting or backdrop of color now. Step into it and explore. What is it you love most about being there? What are you drawn to? Is it the scenery, the activity, the people around you, the wide-open space? Stay there for a few minutes, exploring and remembering . . . What is it that makes you feel most beautiful and free? Are you experiencing freedom now?

PRAY

Father, you have made me—so perfectly, so beautifully—just as you intended. You don't make mistakes. I want to believe that is true; I want to live in the confidence of knowing who I am, in you. I give you the lie that I am not beautiful. I surrender my fear of messing up, my fear of not being perfect. I am not perfect and that is okay. I believe you love me, you love to be with me, you are here, and I am made to live this life moving with you, completely free. In Jesus' name, Amen.

Out of Hiding

IT'S EARLY, LIGHT PEEKING THROUGH cracks in the shades. I tiptoe to the alcove in the family room downstairs, bare toes pressed into the carpet's thick beige wool. I kneel on the floor, hands open in the lap of my flannel pajamas, eyes tired from not enough sleep. My breathing rushes, but I will myself to take a deep, slow breath. Oh, Father, I don't have to do this, do I?

I'm not sure whether to blame Tricia or you. Tricia spent our small group time talking about confession. She said something beautiful happens when we lay bare our heart to community. She said there's freedom when we choose vulnerability rather than fear. But how can I ever speak out loud what I've kept hidden?

When Tricia said those words, my chest tightened and my heart started to pound. I don't want to believe it. Say aloud to friends what I can't even say to you? Oh, God, why is this coming up now? I haven't thought about this for so long. It's been fine, not thinking about it, hasn't it? I can't bear thinking about it. I can't bear thinking about what I did. What good would it do? What good would it ever do to talk about it with other people?

But here we are.

God, I can't do this. Oh, I am remembering it now. *I can't do this.* I can't go back there. It all happened so fast. I was so frustrated. I reacted before I realized what I was doing. I don't want to remember that moment, yet here I am, remembering the scene as if it were a movie. Oh, I hate it. How could I do that? And why? Oh, God, I wish I could rewind it, do it over. I don't deserve forgiveness. Are you shocked, too, by what I did? Jesus, you were obviously far away, and you feel far away now. Is it because of what I did?

I don't see the point of thinking about this anymore. If I tell those women, they are going to hate me, reject me; you know that. Well, maybe they won't hate me, but they will judge me, look at me differently. And I'll never be able to un-tell them. They will know—forever—what kind of person I am. I don't think I could bear that.

I refuse to believe vulnerability is a good thing, at least not when it comes to this. I don't want to think about this anymore. It's ridiculous, really. Can't we just move on?

God?

Please, don't push me. Don't make me to listen to Tricia's words. Isn't it fine, this secret, just between us? This relationship the two of us have, right here, is pretty good, right? I'm fine. I am. I know you love me, that what I've done doesn't change that. So let's just keep going, move past this. Let's keep things like they are, okay?

When we went around the circle last week, I just sat there, wishing we could just change the topic. But then Tricia went first. She shared something I had never known about her, a situation that brings her pain still, but a situation where you, she said, are healing her heart. And then Lisa went next. And then Stacy. It was beautiful, really. They were so brave to share, and I felt so honored to be entrusted with these stories. I loved these friends even more.

Father, are you here with me, right now? The sun is rising. We have our Bible study again today. Will you give me courage? Will you help me tell my story?

MY DARLING, I REACH AROUND NOW, my arms on your shoulders, my chin on your head. I sit here with you, my beloved one. I kneel beside you, wondering if you will take that deep breath now. Yes, that one. Take that deep breath, my love. It is not good to hold everything in.

And now stay. This is you. Claim who you are, my love. Let me help you recognize how I've made you to be. Can you say yes to that again, my love? Can you awake this day and see the sun shining forth? Can you ask me to come and bring newness to your heart?

You have seen where I've been with you. You've heard my whispers. Want to ask for even more of me? Want to let me in even more?

I wait and stay, filling all the spaces where you let me in. You know that place in your heart, in your past that is not yet fully surrendered to me? Let me press here some more, child.

You know where it is, this place where I want to heal you still, more fully—and fill you, even more, with me. I know this place in you. I love you. I hope no part of you wants no part of me.

Let's make this a new season, a season of beginning again, a season of growing again, a season of letting me in again. Let's make this a season where all the old is thrown out. You are beautiful, my darling, and that beauty is more than external.

It is the beauty of your heart that I've claimed, that I've rescued, that I say is yours to use to speak, to teach, to love. For there are daughters in a different season that need you to say yes to this season—this season of rebirth and newness I've given to you. You are shown the freedom that comes with vulnerability, trusting me with your story. You are invited out of hiding, the surrender of pride. There are women who need to hear your story, who will see me in you and be encouraged to step forward, also, into hope and light and freedom. Might that be worship? Might that be being with me? Trust the friends I bring, these sisters. You are safe with me.

I love seasons, the changing and the turning. In the changing there is newness and rebirth.

I am good.

Come and see.

 LISTEN

Picture Elena in the family room, talking to God. Picture her in her Bible study, conflicted. What did she say that resonates with you? What did God say to her that you also needed to hear? Write a prayer to God in response.

THINK

> *Therefore, confess your sins to one another and pray for*
> *one another, that you may be healed. The prayer of a righteous*
> *person has great power as it is working. (James 5:16)*

1. How do you love to connect with God? Can you imagine yourself with him? What do you and he do together?

2. How do you describe the season you are in now? Do you feel close to God? Do you feel far away? Running to him? Running away?

3. What is God inviting you to experience with him in this season? How do you need healing? What is it you've never confessed to anyone and God is asking you to trust him with now?

4. What story is God calling you to share with another person?

 TRUST

Ask God to show you what, in your past, you struggle letting go of—a moment or a memory of something you did that made you feel separate from him. Now imagine Jesus standing before you in this season, saying, "Arise, my love, my beautiful one. Give your burdens to me. Let me make you new." Consider this verse from Song of Solomon: "For behold, the winter is past; the rain is over and gone. The flowers appear on the earth, the time of singing has come, and the voice of the turtledove is heard in our land. The fig tree ripens its figs, and the vines are in blossom; they give forth fragrance. Arise, my love, my beautiful one, and come away" (2:11-13). Picture yourself here, in this scene, with Jesus. How are you responding? What do you do and/or say in response to his invitation to trust him with your story? Stay here for a few minutes; stay present with Jesus in the scene.

 PRAY

Father, I want to be with you. I want to believe you are with me. I lay down all regret about the past. I lay down who I was and who I am. I want to see myself as you see me. Help me to trust that you are safe, that you bring community around me that is safe. Free me from fear of confession. Let me stand before you, unashamed and clean, living in gratitude of your sacrifice, Jesus. In this place of vulnerability, before you, safe in the community that you bring, I live whole. I confess my whole heart to you. I ask for your forgiveness. I am white as snow. In Jesus' name, Amen.

Little Laugh Girl

GOD, I'M GOING TO GET TO THE POINT. You know the words *dutiful*, *faithful*, *trustworthy*, and *strong*? I have aspired to those since I was little. Be the person my family can count on. Be the friend who sticks close. Be the sister who is present and thinks of others more than herself. I try.

My aunt told me once that I have a servant's heart. It sounded like a good thing. So here's my question: Is that what it means for a woman to be your daughter, God? A person who serves? I want to do whatever makes you proud of me, but I wonder if I am doing enough. Are you happy when you look on me? Do I make you smile?

I have a friend who tells me you are a God of joy, of laughter. I'm not sure I've heard you laugh, Father. Can I say that it is difficult for me to imagine you having a sense of humor? Do you find things funny? Do you play? Do you ever laugh when you are with me? I haven't heard you. Could we do that together? Have fun?

Where are you when I'm serving? Are you standing beside me? Are you sitting and leaning close? Are you picking up dishes and whispering in my ear? Where are you at eight o'clock when my patience is gone and I'm wondering how to keep loving people while feeling completely spent? Are your hands on your hips, wishing more of me? Are you in the hallway or the kitchen? Are you just outside the kids' rooms, or leaning, relaxed, on the stairs?

I'm trying to find you, Father. I'm trying.

Maybe I just need to walk even closer with you, Father. I read my Bible. I read books about you. I wake each morning and think about how I can love my family and friends. I don't sleep at night until I have prayed. Is this what I'm supposed to do? Should I do more? What?

I'll try this: I'll give myself to you. I give you my decisions and all my plans. I am yours, my Lord. (Is this what it takes for me to feel you close? Am I doing this right?)

I'll try to wait. I'll try to wait on you.

MY DEAR ONE, I love how you spend time with me. I love how you pursue me. I love how you search for me. Want to do something new? Want to go on an adventure together? What if we went away, just the two of us? It could be quiet, yes, or it could be loud. I know the quiet is not what you love best. But I know you want to hear me more. I know you want to know me more. So what if you took my hand, and I showed you some things about you that I just love?

First, your hands, my darling. Those hands of yours are precious— the way they touch and they hold and they comfort the ones you love and keep them close. Also, your eyes, my darling, sparkle, and I delight in looking at them. They have warmth in them, and when I knit you together, your eyes were a part of you I crafted with care and intention. You use them so beautifully, my dear—how you seek ways to see beyond yourself, how you notice hearts of people who are hurting.

And together, your eyes and hands? With them you love people and show them they are not alone.

And your heart ties all this together; it ties together and makes beautiful the eyes and the hands.

And yes, my girl, this is what makes me laugh. I can't help but jump and run and spin fast with joy when I see you. I can't help but rejoice over you, delight in being with you. Your love is the love I've given you, and the most perfect thing is that you know you can't help but pour this love out. You experience me as you love, as you serve, as you claim and give out the gifts I've given you.

My love, you have been my girl since before you were born. You have been my girl since before you could speak, since before your lips curved into their first smile. I have adored you from the beginning. And the beginning, with me, is always the best place to be, for it is forever.

Beginning. Always. The reason to laugh, to jump, to sing.

 **LISTEN**

Johanna wants to understand God's personality in greater depth. Do you? How do you relate to her? What is your reaction to her conversation with God? What do you want to say to him now? Write your prayer to God here.

THINK

*Be still, and know that I am God. I will be exalted among
the nations, I will be exalted in the earth! (Psalm 46:10)*

1. What do you think it means to please God?

2. In what way do you struggle with striving rather than surrendering? Specifically, what might God be inviting you to surrender to him this week?

3. God speaks to Johanna about the beginning he has for her. What is it? What beginning do you pray he has for you?

 TRUST

Set down everything you are holding. Relax your shoulders. Let your hands fall open at your sides. Picture yourself in an open space, a place of peace and beauty. There is light falling on your face. Jesus approaches you, walking toward you from a distance. He has something in his hands he wants to give you. Let Jesus use your imagination and speak to your heart. What does he invite you to give to him? What does he have for you in return?

 PRAY

Father, you come. You gather me. You remind me I am yours. I confess I forget I don't have to do a thing to be loved by you. You have formed me with your hands; you love me no matter what. Help me loosen my desire for control—trying to run a race you never asked me to run. Let me run beside you; let me rest beside you. I accept your invitation for a new beginning—my abiding in you. Amen.

You are made to move with me, my love.
I sing to you a song your heart knows,
for you are not forgotten. I see you.
I see your beauty. I behold you, and I behold
your light, and I remove the shrouds
so your light can freely shine.

DAPHNE

Legacy

AS THE SEASONS CHANGE, I watch the trees outside my windows. The leaves turn from green to bright orange and red. There is quiet here, in this new place where all six of us moved. We are far from the city now.

The countryside sings tunes sweet and low—the creak of branches in the wind, the frogs when night blankets the hills. There is music here I wish he could hear, too. I miss him. I miss his voice and his smile and the way it felt when his arms were around me. My dad.

He's been gone twenty-one years. Remember how he battled, at home and in and out of hospital rooms, for years? Do you remember how he believed—and we all believed—he would be healed? Do you remember our prayers?

My heart aches for him. He loved me, making me eager to have children and raise them with the love he showed me when I was young. His dying wasn't in my plan.

That daughter of mine is growing up so fast, Father, and I hate that my dad hasn't been here to see her grow. Twenty-one, the same number of years he has been gone. And now she has moved out and is on her own. How can she be grown already? Is this the same little girl I used to carry around and cuddle close? I can hardly believe I've raised these four children and my dad has been gone the whole time.

You have made me strong. Resilient. I know you have given me what I need to raise these children, but I want to hear. Your words are more important to me than any pep talk anyone else could ever give. We've moved so far away, far from the city and the home I knew. It feels right. But I still worry and wonder and hope this is all going to turn out more than fine. I hope for legacy.

God, time is going so fast. I fear I haven't done as good a job as my dad did raising me. So I'm checking in, God, my Father who never leaves. How am I doing? Am I raising these children in a way that would make my dad smile? Are *you* pleased with me?

DARLING, how he loves you. It is an overwhelming love, a true father's love that came from my heart in him. I know what it is like to give up something you love. I know what it means to have a beloved one suffer.

He is no longer where you can speak with him. But I have been present with you. I've never left you. All the hours in the hospital. All the nights you were home alone. All the nights you stayed up late in your room, worrying and wondering how to fix this, how to pray hard enough to make him well.

I know.

I know it was so hard and your heart hurt and you didn't want him to go.

I know.

I give you new beginnings, my daughter. Each time you turn to me, each moment you surrender to me, I begin again in you. I gather you up, my love.

Those were my arms you felt, too, when he held you close. Those were my words of love, too, when he looked you in the eyes and told you it would be okay. He told you he was there; you could tell him anything; he loved you and he would never stop.

That father's love is a fierce love. It is a love that would give anything for his children. And he hated that he wasn't able to keep staying here, loving you. But he knew me, and you know me too. His prayers, again and again, were prayers of love for you. Prayers of yearning for you. Prayers of desire on your behalf.

He loved you so much, he surrendered you to me, again and again and again.

Those children of yours? They are love passed down, my darling. That love he showed you? That love I gave to him? You are showing it to your children. You are blessed with my presence. You are blessed with my love in you. You are blessed with my hope in you. Our family legacy is love, and you have richly added to it.

Well done.

Well, *well* done.

You've made both your fathers very proud.

 LISTEN

Daphne mourns the loss of her dad and worries that she will not carry on his legacy of loving and raising her children well. What is the legacy Daphne inherits from God? What do you want to tell God in response to this conversation?

THINK

> *When the righteous cry for help, the L*ORD *hears and delivers*
> *them out of all their troubles. The L*ORD *is near to the brokenhearted*
> *and saves the crushed in spirit. Many are the afflictions of the righteous,*
> *but the L*ORD *delivers him out of them all. He keeps all his bones;*
> *not one of them is broken. (Psalm 34:17–20)*

1. What loss have you experienced that has had a significant effect on your life?

2. In what ways do you need reassurance that you are doing okay?

3. What questions do you have for God now? How do you need him to come and speak to your heart?

 TRUST

Consider this statement from Thomas Merton: "If you want to identify me, ask me not where I live, or what I like to eat, or how I comb my hair, but ask me what I think I am living for, in details, and ask me what I think is keeping me from living fully for the thing I want to live for."[1]

For what are you living? What is keeping you from living fully? Write a prayer to God, in detail, telling him the legacy you hope to inherit from him . . . the legacy you want to leave for those coming after you.

PRAY

Father, I give to you the legacy of my family, of my friendships, of my relationships. I want to leave a legacy that is beautiful, that represents your love for me. I trust you with my life; I trust that I can turn to you for wisdom and strength and hope and everything I need. You are already proud of me. And it is in that confidence that I live and love. In Jesus' name, Amen.

---

1. Thomas Merton, *My Argument with the Gestapo* (New Directions, 1975), 160–161.

Moving Toward Home

BROWN CARDBOARD STACKS SILENT like morose soldiers awaiting marching orders. Everything we own is shoehorned inside them. It's taken days to pack . . . but weeks to admit I want to scream and tear open those boxes and chuck plates and books and toys across the room.

We're saying good-bye to the house we thought you gave us, God, the house of our dreams, the one we worked so hard for, the one we thought we'd live in forever. Why? Why now? Why this job loss? Why these financial struggles?

The worst day was telling the kids we had to move. Dillon lowered his eyes like a puppy dog. Sam slammed her door and didn't talk to me for four days.

We collected boxes from the supermarket. Went to the produce section, but were sent around back. Stacks of banana boxes and apple boxes. And then we went to the neighbors and collected plastic containers they said they didn't need.

We aren't moving far. The rental house is just a few blocks down past the school, and then another right turn at the donut shop next to the Starbucks where I used to go before work. But you know all these details, God. And I'm trying not to be mad at you, but I really thought we were in the clear. I thought the work would keep coming, especially for John. We had worked hard for so many years to buy our own house. And then to foreclose? To have to give it back and move out and squeeze into another house that doesn't feel like home?

But you know what is hurting most.

You know.

John isn't talking much anymore. I think he's seriously depressed, God. Darkness covers him; he's convinced he's failed us somehow. I wonder if he fears I respect him less because he lost his job. It doesn't help that the whole family acts like the world has turned upside down.

I know we don't deserve a thing, Father. I know you provide everything we need. I know you give and you take away. I know I should trust you more here.

But it might be awhile until I feel okay again. I'm trying to have faith, to believe light can shine someday soon. It feels impossible to have faith, though, when I want to just yell at you and scream, "Why?"

Why?

THE ROOM FEELS SILENT, daughter, and you wonder if I am here.

I am.

I hear the prayers, my love. I collect the tears in the night, measure the sobs of John, Dillon, Sam. I feel the confusion, the accusations, the fear.

You think dreams are being ripped away—all the things you worked so hard for. Gone are the expectations for the hard work, the realization of what you believe you've earned. It's time to let go of those old dreams so I can give you new ones. Don't stay looking back, filled with regret. It isn't helping now. John is going to be okay, if he surrenders, too. It is time to trust the future I have for your family more than the temporary things you and John have worked so hard to achieve.

Come home.

No, your dreams are not being stolen. No, I am not taking something from you to replace it with something worse, although I know it feels that way. I am good. My plans are good. You can't see what I see ahead. Trusting me is hard. But I will help you trust me. And if you trust in me more than in your circumstances, you will see the new dreams, the new home I move you toward.

And it's not just a physical place I have for you, Melissa.

Come home.

Come with me, now, to where I want to take you. Sometimes moving is more than a move to a new physical place. Sometimes the move is me asking you to move deeper with me, to come closer in. I know you are filled with uncertainty, but you are okay. Keep your eyes on me. Look to me. I show you how to see.

I have a light that shines bright, my love, and I shine it forth, marking the way ahead. I shine it for Sam and for Dillon. I shine it for John. I shine it for you. Listen for me in your art, in your work, in how you love and serve.

Come home.

Stay here, where I am, where I shine bright the light. Stay here, where I am, and I will direct you and bring forth hope in the dark places—all the dark places where fear wants you to sink further in.

I lift you out, my love.

Yes, keep your eyes on me. Here is home.

 **LISTEN**

Melissa cries out to God, angry, worried, and scared. What is happening to her home, her family, is not what she planned. How does Melissa's conversation with God resonate with you? What do you want to say to God in response?

THINK

> *He who dwells in the shelter of the Most High will abide in*
> *the shadow of the Almighty. I will say to the Lord, "My refuge and*
> *my fortress, my God, in whom I trust." For he will deliver you from*
> *the snare of the fowler and from the deadly pestilence. He will cover*
> *you with his pinions, and under his wings you will find refuge;*
> *his faithfulness is a shield and buckler. You will not fear the terror*
> *of the night, nor the arrow that flies by day. (Psalm 91:1–5)*

1. What brings Melissa the most fear? What is prompting her anger, her hurt, her confusion? How can you relate to her?

2. When have you felt angry at God? Will you give God your frustration, your fear, and your anger?

3. How does God respond to Melissa? How does he encourage her in the midst of doubt and uncertainty? What uncertainties are you facing in your life? How is God asking you to move toward him—to come home—and trust him right now?

TRUST

Reread Psalm 91:1–5: "He who dwells in the shelter of the Most High will abide in the shadow of the Almighty. I will say to the Lord, 'My refuge and my fortress, my God, in whom I trust.' For he will deliver you from the snare of the fowler and from the deadly pestilence. He will cover you with his pinions, and under his wings you will find refuge; his faithfulness is a shield and buckler. You will not fear the terror of the night, nor the arrow that flies by day."

Read the verses slowly and reflectively. Consider what parts of the verses stand out to you. Meditate on the words that stood out to you most. Read the verses aloud again. Consider how they are speaking to you. Which words resonate the most? Underline them. Ask God what it is about these words that he wants you to consider more deeply—and understand and know.

Spend a few minutes praying to God, speaking back to him what you believe he is trying to tell you.

 PRAY

Father, in my prayers filled with questions, you offer me truth and wisdom and love through your Word, although you don't always point me to specific answers. I want to be okay with that—okay with trusting in you and in who you are, even though I may not understand everything about my circumstances. Help me to be okay with not knowing the why of things, and to be content, instead, with knowing the One who knows all the whys and has everything under his control. You've got me. I know it. I am safe under your wings. Let me rest in who you are. Amen.

Beyond Where Time Touches

AS A CHILD, I learned about you. Every afternoon, for months, I curled up next to my grandmother when she was sick. She showed me the pages of her Bible, worn and beautiful, her loopy cursive filling the margins of the Psalms—and Romans and Hebrews, too. She said love is surprising—that it doesn't always look like we think it's supposed to, but it's the only sure thing to believe in. I didn't understand her then, but I think I'm beginning to now.

In the examination room where I have my second round of mammograms, I glimpse your surprising love. There have been so many surprises, of course—small, normal moments when I've needed you most: in the friends surrounding me when my sister died, in the lifeguard scooping up our daughter from the swimming pool when she was two. I can only imagine all the other moments—the moments you've rescued and I never realized you were there.

The exam room is tiny, with white linoleum and a coffee table in the dark corner—and a wooden lamp casting warm yellow light under a cream, linen shade. It is a lamp that is easier to imagine in a living room with a retro velvet couch decorated with textured throw pillows from Anthropologie and a shelf of hardback books with pretty covers. It doesn't belong in this room, this exam room with tall computers on rolling carts and gigantic x-ray equipment that determine one of two kinds of news: "everything looks good" or "this looks suspicious." I appreciate the gesture. Someone tried to make the room cheery during the wait.

While I wait, I cross my legs and hold my bare elbows with my hands, trying to keep the open-in-front, salmon polyester cape wrapped around me. It feels silly now, remembering how I pulled on my favorite jeans and slipped on canvas wedges for the afternoon appointment. I even blow-dried my hair and put on makeup. Small comfort, I guess, when everything else feels out of my control.

I sit in the cushioned exam room chair and think about how, in this moment, for all I know, I am perfectly fine. I could be sick, or I could be healthy. I wonder how many more minutes I will sit waiting, and how surreal it is, being in this dim room by myself, waiting for news that might change how I will live my life. "Your X-rays came back negative." "We need to run a few more tests." But I want to decide how I will live from now on, before I get the news. I think about how you love me, how you are with me. I decide that nothing any doctor can say will change what I believe about love, how I think about you.

Eventually, the technician comes in with a friendly smile, calls me "darling," and asks me to follow her to a different room down the hall where the radiologist will do an ultrasound. She says the doctor will come in to talk to me after that. I pick up my purse and carry it in front of me, hugging my hands to my chest. Here I am, in another dim, tiny room, this time with an exam table near the wall. I lie on the table and stare at the ceiling.

MY LOVE FOR YOU is not temporary. I stay, in the deeper place, and am present in all the moments you live. Moments such as those in the exam room, when you sit and find me, are a turning over of your heart; my power in you is released.

You choose truth—believing your life is more than what can be measured by dates on a calendar or by the movement of a clock. Because you choose truth, you experience my love without bound-aries. There are no boundaries to me, you see. And you get to spend your life choosing to see me within boundaries or beyond them.

I know you don't know what is coming with these medical results, but I do. Keep your heart aligned with mine. I am here, Samantha. I am here.

I am in all places and in all moments and in all things. But so much is hidden from you—both difficult and good. You can rarely see the details. Yet remember this: You can imagine me. You can hold onto me. May I help you imagine more of what I can see? May I help you let go of restrictions about what life is supposed to look like, the limits of a day, a measurement of tangible time?

With me, time isn't tangible, is it? I show up in moments because I love you. I show you where I am because I love you. I don't show you all things, all the places and moments where I am, because I am teaching you faith. I am teaching you to rely on and trust in more than what you can feel and hear and see.

You're going to have to break faith wide open, my strong one. This means you're going to have to stay in the place where time does not touch—all while living on the tangible earth and with the people I love and created. Since there is more here than what you can see, you must trust me with what you can't see. And you must also want to see what you cannot.

My power will equip you to love with my love. It will give you strength and offer hope to the children who are stuck in the moments they think they can measure with a device, a list, a diploma, a degree. And this is where you will find me, too, where time cannot touch you. Remain in love, where I stay.

 LISTEN

Samantha, in a posture of waiting for her results from the doctor, recognizes God's love for her. When you read Samantha's prayer and God's response, what was your reaction? How do you feel about waiting when you have reason to be concerned? How do you feel about God's response to Samantha? Write your own prayer to God.

 THINK

I wait for the Lord, my soul waits, and in his word I hope;
my soul waits for the Lord more than watchmen for the morning,
more than watchmen for the morning. (Psalm 130:5-6)

1. What is your greatest challenge when it comes to waiting on God?

2. In what way do you struggle with letting go of control? How do you struggle, right now, with what you can't see?

3. How do you want to see and trust God more this week?

4. God speaks of his love transcending time. What line above, in his response, resonates with you most?

TRUST

Consider how you are waiting on God, and imagine your own waiting room, although not necessarily a medical one. So this room might be your kitchen, your living room, your car, your bedroom … whatever is appropriate for the kind of waiting you are doing right now. Picture yourself there, waiting on God. How do you feel about waiting on him? What thoughts are going through your head?

Now grab a piece of paper and a pen and draw a line down the middle of the paper. On the left side of the paper write down the emotions that you feel when you are waiting on God. Then look up five of the following verses. On the right side of your paper, write down the truth about how God blesses us when we trust him, beyond our circumstances, in our waiting.

- Hope: Psalm 33:20; 39:7
- Strength and courage: Psalm 27:14; 31:24
- Trust in his holy name: Psalm 33:21
- His unfailing love: Psalm 33:18,22
- Patience: Psalm 37:7; 40:1; Habakkuk 3:16; Romans 8:25; Hebrews 6:15
- Peace in our hearts: Lamentations 3:26
- Assurance that he is all we need, he is our portion: Lamentations 3:24
- Obedience: Psalm 37:34; 119:166; Isaiah 26:8-9
- Desire for him: Isaiah 26:8-9
- Eagerness: Romans 8:19,23
- Single-mindedness: Psalm 62:5
- Expectation: Psalm 123:2; Micah 7:7

- Belief in his Word: Psalm 130:5
- Steadfastness: Hosea 12:6
- Joy: John 3:29

 PRAY

Father, I give you the things I cannot control, everything that is ahead. You give me the choice to trust you or be overwhelmed with fear. You give me the choice to trust what I see or what I do not see. You are good and beyond any boundaries of time and space. Help me to see more, see the tangible ways you are here and the intangible. In Jesus' name, Amen.

Strings

FINGERS STIFF, WRISTS SORE. Up all night practicing, cello heavy against my chest. This stage hasn't been swept in weeks. Dust blankets my scuffed black boots. I pull my hair back and square my shoulders to the wooden frame. Deep breath, yawn. I'm tired, but Lord, there is music in me I need to play.

My grandfather taught me these notes, his fingers, thick and calloused, wrapping around the back of my hand. His arms encircled me and the cello, too. Music I first learned to speak, the bend of bow upon grandpa's cello strings my first words. He played in the sunroom off the kitchen, where the light would stream and warm the oak floors. I had been peeking from the kitchen doorway, a plastic baton my bow and a shoebox my cello.

When Grandpa paused playing, his gray head lifting up and his brown eyes meeting mine, he invited me into a sacred space. Music was more than notes or rhythm or song there. It was *magic*. He lifted me onto his lap, took my hands in his, let my fingers run lightly over the strings. He cupped my hands and placed them on the bow. Together we played, his fingers over mine, the vibrations of music becoming my true song, the one I knew how to sing.

These memories, Father, the first ones, are more than memories of a little girl on the lap of her grandfather who loved her. They are more than moments cherished from a past, minutes and then hours in a room where music became what filled the space— more than light, more than color, more than anything I could see with my eyes. It must be heaven, Father.

The music carries me to beauty. It carries me to you. It overwhelms me, lifting me to the place where I am myself, and I am beautiful. It is where I am yours; it is where I am with you. The long glissandos; the staccato runs plucked from that rich place where notes are born; the bell-like harmonics, gently pulled from the secret spots of the strings; the double stops like the voices of a grandfather and a little girl, singing different notes of the same ancient song.

Even in times of sorrow, there is joy here, in this place of music with you. Even in the unknowns and things I cannot control, I am filled. You have placed music inside me, and I see it, and I hear it, and my whole self rises and sees you. Here is where I want to stay.

Help me teach my students these notes, Father. Can I do it— invite them to love it like my grandfather invited me? It isn't just music from their hands, their ears, their arms and minds they need to play. There is music within them you want them to know. And when I am with you, and I remember my grandfather, and I lower my head, close my eyes, and let these children hear the music, too, I see how some of them are awakening to the music. They are beginning to know this place—future heaven whispered now—with you.

Soon they'll be coming up onto this stage, Father. And I will teach them what you teach me. So come and fill up this space with your music, your whole resonant self, that we may hear it, and see it, and smell it, and taste it. Let us *be* in it, Father. We want to be in you, God, letting the songs in our hearts resound loud and long. It is the music of your lullabies, the music of majesty, the music of hope, the music of sacrifice and wonder and beauty and all possibility unfolding over and over again. You never end, God. You are what we need most. One note, then another.

I will stay here, playing, until my fingers cannot move and my arms lift no more.

I CLOSE MY EYES and see you. I close my eyes and hear you. I know what you sound like. I know the colors of your music. I know how song resounds when love is the key.

You know love song, don't you, my dearest? You know how I stay here, with you. You know how I captured you in my arms, wrapped you up so tight in the grasp of a grandfather who loved you, just like I held him in my arms and taught him the notes of my song, too.

Let me keep writing notes upon your heart, my love. I play them there, open strings and then chords, impossible for human hands to reach. You know each of these children? Let me show you what their songs sound like. Let me show what the songs look like through my eyes. To be in the music, you must know how you are loved.

These children are here to learn love song, and you can teach it to them—not only through the music on the cello you play, but through your smile, your laughter, your instruction and patience and guidance. Show them how music is within them when they know they are loved, and they are known, and they are held, and my arms never stop wrapping them around.

Show them *me*, child.

I listen here. I lean in here, eyes closed, seeing you—hearing the song of your heart and the songs each of my children are made to play. The scrape of the bow, the playing lilt of the strings—I adore each run, each sighing rise of the melody.

Play loud these songs, the music that is written in you. When you play it, you know me. When you hear it, you see me. When you are in it, everyone else around you wants the music within themselves, too. And then they rise, and they are prompted to open up the door when I knock, and I have for them music played upon the notes of their hearts—music they are meant, with their whole lives, to play.

 LISTEN

Veronica reflects on one of the biggest influences on her life: her grandfather teaching her music. Playing music is how she worships God. What relationship has changed your life? What do you like to do with God? Write a prayer to God telling him about it.

THINK

He put a new song in my mouth, a song of praise to our God.
Many will see and fear, and put their trust in the LORD. (Psalm 40:3)

1. What do you love to do in God's presence that makes you feel the most alive, energized, and fulfilled?

2. Or if you don't yet know what you love to do as a way to worship him, stop and pray, asking him to show you.

3. What does God say to Veronica that you feel he is also saying to you?

 ## TRUST

Find a song that articulates–either in words, the melody, or both–the music you feel represents your relationship with God right now. This can be the song you want to sing to him, or the song you feel he sings to you, or the song that makes you feel wistful for him, or the song that helps you imagine what it is like to be in his presence. Play it, over and over. Let this be the truth your heart wants to express to your Father. Stay here, singing it to him–or with him. Look for him as you listen. Listen for his voice as you see.

PRAY

Father, I am uniquely and perfectly made. Because I am designed by you, I am made to worship you with my whole heart, my whole body, my whole life. Help me figure out how I am designed, uniquely, to worship you. Let the words of my mouth sing praise and the actions of my heart demonstrate your Spirit within me. You are glorious and good, and I surrender everything that gets in the way of me living a life of worship. Show me how I hold back. Help me not. Let my whole heart be yours. In Jesus' name, Amen.

REBECCA

Resolution

IT WAS THE WAY he looked at me.

Before he even said a word, I knew. His eyes said it: I was the last one he expected to see doing the photo shoot, camera in my hand. He must have guessed I was one of the assistants—a girl who fetched coffee, one of the clean-up crew.

Do you remember how he said it? "Hey—uh, Becky—is that your name? Tell the photographer to hurry up. Oh, and can you get more half-and-half over here? I've got to get going after this. I need some cream for my espresso, and I really hope we can get this shoot over within the next thirty minutes."

I was livid, but I kept it under control. "I *am* the photographer, Mr. Anderson. This is my studio. Your company arranged this appointment for you with me. I'll have my assistant get you what you need."

I guess I'm not able to hide it from you, am I, God? My howling, righteous rage. My desire to smash the coffee pot across his balding head.

Sorry. But you know my anger, Father. I've heard it a thousand times, from a hundred Mr. Andersons—the condescension, the assumptions. I can almost see the half-formed syllogism clouding his brain: *Becky is a woman. Becky's skin's darker than mine. Ergo, Becky exists to fetch my creamer.*

Becky isn't your errand-girl, sir.

I ask my assistant, Robert, to buy more creamer. Mr. Anderson shouts after him to "*pleeeeeeease* make *suuuuuure* it's *orgaaaaanic.*" How long, oh Lord? How freakin' long?

Reading my light meter now, gauging the levels in the room. They're worse than I'd like. I know I'm angry. I just get tired of people assuming who and what I am with half a glance, who or what I'm not with the other half. I'm me. A woman. With dark skin and an accent. With a studio and an international portfolio that kicks you-know-just-what, Lord. I've worked for it. My family worked to set me up for it. My dad washing cars during the day, helping the night shift janitor at the high school at night. Paid on the side. He was the one who kept the family together after Mom had to go. Ten years ago, she called us from Mexico, not sure if she could ever get a green card. God, you see who each of us really is. You love us for who we can fully be.

And some people just can't ever see past their own creamer.

The door slams behind Robert, sending echoes through the bare studio. Mr. Anderson's head snaps up from his screen. It's time. I breathe deep. Put my eye to the viewfinder.

You really do see, don't you, Lord?

Focus.

Click.

YES, FAIR ONE.

Yes, I see. Every false and broken category, every prejudice, every injustice. I see the large and the small evils, the daily unfairness. I see the sin and pride—in him and in you—and I see the good things in you both as well. You know I hate the labels, the categories, the grading. I hate every self-importance. I call every son and daughter priceless, and seethe when they put price tags on each other.

I am sorry, Rebecca. I hate that you live in a world that doesn't know me fully. It is not fair that you have to fight to prove you are more than what people have decided they see. I like that fight in you—how you refuse to believe you are less just because someone else believes he or she is more. But to be free, I need you to give your frustration, your anger, and your pain to me. Come to me with your longing for justice. I hear you, and I fight with you—for justice for sons and for daughters. I fight for all the ones I love.

It's going to be a long road, this resolution, this justice. But it's coming.

I suppose you could still smash that pot over his head, but I have a better idea.

Together, let's resolve to open his mind. With the truth. With the love.

Together.

 **LISTEN**

Rebecca asks God what he thinks about the sexism and racism she experiences. What did you think about Rebecca's prayer to God and his response? Write a prayer telling him what you want to say.

THINK

Beloved, never avenge yourselves, but leave it to the wrath of God, for it is written, "Vengeance is mine, I will repay, says the Lord." (Romans 12:19)

1. Rebecca is angry and frustrated due to prejudice against women and minorities. How have you witnessed or experienced this personally in your life?
2. How does God explain prejudice?
3. In what specific way in your life are you longing for justice to come?

 TRUST

Get in a place where you feel comfortable, where you are unself-conscious and uninhibited. Play music, if you'd like. Spend some time letting yourself be present in this moment with God. Ask him to show you his perspective on injustice in your life—whether you've received it or been unjust to others yourself. Stay here. Listen to what he has to say.

PRAY

Father, let me crawl up into your lap and feel your arms around me. Let me hear what you have to say. I want to trust you and go to you with any question, any concern. Help me know you more. Help me want to be with you—calm, relaxed, talking to you like you are my protector, a listener, a friend. Tell me again you have me, you are with me, you are so happy I am your daughter. In your Son's name, Amen.

Is it really dark here, now, my love?
Is the wind so loud you can't hear me?
Is the night so dark you can't see me?
Is the storm so great you can't find me?
You are found, my love.
You are always found, I say.

Where Story Begins

WIND DANCES LIKE BUTTERFLIES through branches laden with crimson, persimmon, and sun. It catches stray hairs framing my face, tickling my nose and resting just above where my eyelashes curl. I reach and pull the hair back behind my ears and close my eyes to hear the wind's song.

It's now been four years since I moved up here with my grandparents. My parents are visiting tomorrow. They'll say they hardly recognize me, I'm sure. It's their favorite thing to say. I still have the tattoos on my arm—the eagle wings on my right shoulder that I got after high school (not their favorite). But the cross on the back of my neck is new. I got that my first year here. But no one can see it when my hair is down.

It's taken these four years living here after high school to make me feel like I might be able to return. Sharing my past with a friend has actually made a difference. Thanks for Drew, God.

It took me a while to trust her, didn't it? But we always seemed to get scheduled the same shift. I bet you did that, didn't you? She'd small talk. I hated it at first. It's hard to explain to her how in the world I ended up here on the mountain passing lattes to tourists. But then there was the day I decided to tell her the truth about me.

In the storage room I lifted up the hem on the left side of my T-shirt a couple of inches and showed her the scars where I used to cut my skin. My parents were the only ones who had seen them—the lines faded now, barely pink. Drew didn't flinch, and in that second we became friends.

We walked to my grandparents' cabin, tucked away in the pines up at the end of the winding dirt road. We sat on the dusty steps of the porch and I told her about high school. I had been overwhelmed by the pressure—AP tests, friends, *not*-friends. I nearly killed myself prepping for the SATs. My stomach ached constantly and I got headaches most afternoons. I was convinced that I didn't really have what it would take to be successful, but cared too much to stop trying.

I told Drew about spring finals week my junior year, how I had bent open a paper clip and tore a gash in my side. The pain was electric. It always woke me up, centered me. It was focus on being my best, and punishment for being a "failure," all in one.

Do you remember how I was doing it a few times a week, using a pen, a pocketknife from my dad's camping cache, whatever? I prided myself on the symmetry of the lines—the grooves in my skin, fairly straight, horizontal, even. One thing about me felt in order.

A year later, my mom caught me. I'd forgotten to lock my door. Or maybe you opened it. My back was to her. I noticed her reflection in my mirror before I could hide what I was doing. She'd only seen a second's worth, but she was already crying.

She didn't say a word; she just held me. I squirmed, pulled back in shock at it all. Then I let her do it. We collapsed to the floor, and I sobbed, too. "I can't do it anymore," was all I could say, again, and again, and again.

I told Drew it was you, God, who was really holding me.

I don't think of coming here as running away anymore. Yes, I was running away from the senseless pressure, from the whole put-together, straight-As achievement circus of it all. But now I see that I was running to you. There was never an away, never a backwards. Only running toward you.

I wait for my parents to arrive, following a trail to a meadow out behind the cabin. And then I walk higher, where the trail curves up, into wind sending leaves jumping and crunching. Wind brushing my cheeks and kissing where light warms skin. Wind pushing against bare skin as I rise, my feet treading sure. One foot, and then another, leaving the carpets of moss, deep velvet green.

I am here, Father, walking the path. My hands empty, fingers bare. But ready for you.

I consecrate my mind, my body, my future. I consecrate my ideas, my dreams, my talents and vision to follow you. I reject the lies I have believed, and I accept that I am your daughter of wisdom. Your daughter of beauty. Your daughter of gentleness and courage and light. I am more than people see, and I claim the new life you give me. I am more than my secret scars. I reject the lie that happiness is measured by the world's achievements. You fill me with your truth.

Say the word—and I will run even closer to you.

YES, RUN TO ME. You are right—you were always running here. To the place beyond achievement, the place where I simply smile at you and say that I am pleased.

There is a great lie stalking the world. It whispers that the value of a woman lies in what she's seen to do. Grades, salaries, awards—and a host of other good things, twisted until the life they might have held is dead and rotten.

It is my life that enlivens, my will that makes you alive, my love that gives you your glittering worth.

And my promise is sure. I will give you more of me, daughter.

You have come many miles, but you have many miles yet to run. You are filled with strength I give you, but you will no longer be held down. I send angels, my daughter. They have surrounded you. They have not left you. And my Holy Spirit in you equips you to speak truth to the young women who need to hear the truth, too. You have felt alone. But you will encourage thousands.

Now arise and run, and tell them this:

"You are more than what you can see. You are more than the world says you are. You are not made like another. What you are given to do, no one else can do like you can. You are wild and brave and unashamed and able.

"You are the Lord's Beloved."

 **LISTEN**

Aliza's trials of struggling to achieve in this world came with a price. But now she sees God's intervention, and good plan for her, too. What do you want to pray in response? Write your prayer.

 THINK

You have made known to me the paths of life;
you will make me full of gladness with your presence. (Acts 2:28)

1. What has been your biggest struggle in trying to fit in with this world?

2. How do you feel about opening your heart to all that God has for you? Is this an invitation you appreciate . . . or does it make you uncomfortable . . . or both?

3. Aliza awakens to God and surrenders the lies she has been believing about achievement and success. How have you struggled in situations that felt out of your control?

 TRUST

Go to a quiet place. Grab your journal and a pen, if you want. Or simply close your eyes and don't write a thing. Imagine your true home in God. Picture the new chapter of life with him that he is inviting you into—beyond your own achievement. What do you want it to look like, sound like? How do you want to feel when you are there? Spend five to ten minutes in solitude, soaking it up, imagining what it will be like to be here, being brave and whole with him.

PRAY

Father, how you see me and where you invite me to go with you are more beautiful than I can imagine. And you invite me deeper into your heart, offering me a place to inhabit with you—a place of freedom and abundance and beauty. No matter how I spend my days, I can be present with you, awake to your presence, awake to possibility, the reality of living in faith. I surrender the things I do not know and do not understand so I can cling all the more tightly to the reality of your love for me, a love always with me, living in me. In Jesus' name, Amen.

RACHEL

Light in the Dark

THIS WASN'T THE PLAN, God.

I don't know why it had to happen this way. Things got so complicated. I didn't think he would really leave. We had dreams and plans. I thought I knew where we were going. I thought I knew who I was, what I was doing. I thought this love you gave us would sustain us, would carry us through anything.

Why, Father, didn't this marriage last?

I am tired, Father, and I am confused. I think I'm mad at you, or at him, or at myself, or at this life. Why, God? Why did it have to be this way? Why did you let this happen? I know you are here, that you are bigger than anything I face, that you are good and you are present in all circumstances. I know you made me, and you bring forth love, even when it seems, for love, there is no way.

I miss love, God. I miss the way it held me. I miss the way it looked at me. I miss the way it made me feel safe and protected. I want to feel safe again at night, God. And I don't feel safe now. It's been a long time since I've felt safe.

Wake me up to what you have, Father. I am tired of sleeping

alone. I am tired of staying in this dark place. The darkness feels so loud and so silent, all at once. I am lonely, and I am scared.

My kids are scared too, God. I don't know what to tell them, how to tell them it will all be okay when I don't know how all this is going to turn out. Can you help me tell them, God? Can you help me tell them it will all be okay, give me words to help them believe it?

Are you present?

Are you sovereign?

Can you complete me?

Heal me?

I LIFT THE HAIR COVERING YOUR FACE, your hair falling forward, covering the beauty I made. You are beauty here, even in this pain. You are carried and you are whole, even here, in this broken place.

For when you are broken, and you are worn, I carry you. And the pieces of you, the ones that feel scattered all over the floor, are the pieces of beauty that I collect, that I've known, that I restore. You know only I make beauty, don't you?

My darling, I am here. You are not alone. And in the night, in the place where the quiet is loud, I come and whisper lullabies in your ear. I speak them straight to your heart, the ones I've sung to you since before you were born.

Let me show you light in a new way. Let me show you light in dark places, the places where pieces of brokenness form mosaics of beauty that never existed on their own. For I am beauty, my darling.

I am beauty, in you.

And let me give you glimpses of what's coming. It is good. And I don't leave you, my darling, in the darkness, in the quiet, in the pain.

I know your every ache, your every question. I hear your every cry. There is no condemnation. Do you believe I bring newness? Do you believe I bring hope?

Let me come into the dark places you've tucked away, far away, the ones I see and you've wanted to keep hidden. I can bring light to memories. I can bring light to future plans. I can bring light to dreams and show you how to dream again.

Keep dreaming, my love. Keep hoping, my love. Keep listening for love songs, for love is safe with me. This love is in your friends, your family, your neighbors. Do you want your heart to be healed? Do you believe I am here? I can show you how, even in the places of pain in the past, I was there.

And beauty shows up in dark places.

Even there.

Even here.

 **LISTEN**

Rachel calls out to God, asking if he is here with her. She is hurting, and the only thing she knows to do is lay herself down, trusting him more than herself. How are you feeling? What is your prayer to God right now?

 THINK

Uphold me according to your promise, that I may live,
and let me not be put to shame in my hope! (Psalm 119:116)

1. How do you need God to bring newness to your life? How do you pray God brings light to dark places? What are those dark places? How do you pray he shines his light?

2. We each need rescue. Do you believe God comes to rescue you? How have you seen God rescue you in the past?

3. What are your raw and honest questions for God?

 TRUST

Rachel hears God tell her, "I am here. You are not alone." Can you believe this applies to your own life, too? How do you feel alone? Where? Picture yourself there, in that place where you feel alone. Ask Jesus to show up in that place. Ask the Holy Spirit to come into that situation with you and reveal his presence, how his light can shine, even in the dark.

PRAY

Father, you come for me in the night and I see you. In this night of uncertainty and fear, I pray you would come and rescue your dear one. Remind me of your presence in all things, in all moments. Rescue me and sustain me. I am held by you, my safe place. You are my light. I am never alone. Thank you. Amen.

Running Shoes and Surrender

MY SHIFT AT THE CAFÉ just ended. My pores smell like coffee beans.

I exit the break room, my hair pulled back into a tighter ponytail, my running shoes laced. I'm ready to go. It's the best part of the day, I now realize. Running home with you.

Are you ready for this? I feel like talking today, while we run. Brace yourself; this conversation is going to be a little different this time.

Ready?

Are you sure?

Okay, here it is.

Father, bring it on.

I want all of you, and I hope you hold nothing back. I can take it; I can go back to those hard moments, those moments when I felt like my world was spinning out-of-control, when I was overwhelmed, when I felt lost and stressed and alone.

I'm convinced I'm ready. I'm convinced I'm tired of trying to hold myself together. I'm convinced I no longer want to do things on my own.

I'm ready for you to heal me. I'm ready to try and trust you more. Will you stay close and lead me to the places I never let you take me before?

You know I've never heard your voice aloud. You know I've never seen your face. But I want to. I'm no longer afraid to pursue you. I'm no longer afraid of surrender. I'm no longer afraid of what from my past you will invite me to see.

Here it is: I'm done being afraid.

Come, Father, meet me now. Come, Jesus, let me keep pace with you. Come, Holy Spirit, fill me; help me listen for you. I believe it is healing you most want me to see.

I want to be bold and fearless with you. I want to stand tall, letting your words to me in that stiff Bible at home be the truth I eat and believe.

Oh come on, Father. Come on in. I am choosing you, no matter what it requires. I want to run right with you. I am tired of running away.

I AM HERE, CHILD. I always wait as long as it takes. I always wait as long as you need me to wait. I've been in no hurry. I've not been worried about your next step. But I do know the next step you should take. And I do know how each step takes you in a direction toward what is good for you, or toward distraction.

When I speak to you, child—because yes, I speak to you—it is to the daughter whom I see underneath the weights you carry. You are strong, my love, in spite of them, because of them. But you should run free.

Oh, daughter, I love that you let me free you; you are not meant to carry these. Heavy. Dark. They hold you back.

Yes, for more of me, for the lightening of your load, for freedom from doubt and worry and chasing; yes, let me run with you.

I hear you. I am coming. I am going to heal in you these places that have not yet seen light. I love your readiness, my darling girl. I love your willingness, my daughter. I love your soft heart and your courage, letting me be your courage and the director of your future now. I lift what you carry, endless strength and speed and stamina. The world is a road unfolding.

You are alive, and becoming more alive.

Run!

You will not grow weary.

 **LISTEN**

Shelby wants God to help her open her whole heart to him. How do you feel about Shelby's attitude? What do you want to say now to God?

_____

_____

_____

_____

_____

_____

_____

_____

_____

_____

_____

_____

_____

_____

_____

_____

_____

_____

_____

_____

THINK

Submit yourselves therefore to God.
Resist the devil, and he will flee from you. (James 4:7)

1. When you hear the word "surrender," what images come to mind? What do you think surrender requires? What would it require of you?

2. What shrouds might you be wearing? What light do you believe has only been allowed to peek through?

3. What freedom does God want to give you now?

 TRUST

Get in a comfortable position, in a chair you love sitting in, or lean back on a pillow on the floor. (Or maybe take a run?) Take a deep breath. In just a moment, close your eyes. Imagine actually holding what you need to surrender, physically, in your hands. Imagine handing these things over to Jesus. One-by-one. Slowly. See him taking them– each person or memory or wound. Watch him then lift off of you the pieces of your shroud. You now shine radiant and white and bright. Sister, you are beautiful. Now close your eyes.

PRAY

Father, I surrender my whole heart. I want to hold nothing back from you. I want to hide no longer. I want to step out, in your light, and receive all that you have for me. You are good, and you have good for me. You have healing for me. Give me courage and hope in you. Let me now experience the joy that comes with knowing surrender is the beginning of life. Thank you, Jesus, for your surrender. Help me accept your life in me and surrender my life, too. In your name, Amen.

SOPHIE

Fresh Air in Night

I HAVE A VISION IN the night.

I watch her walking. Sure, with authority, like grass swaying in gentle wind. Is she so different from me? More beautiful? She goes forward, knowing with each step she is not alone, but held. Eyes straight ahead, shoulders determinedly set. She is looking. And she is seeing. Hands calloused and strong. She looks for the lost, knowing her King walks with her, before her, knowing she is led.

She is beautiful. Beauty walking. Who can follow her? Who can follow beauty into the night? Who can follow her onto the paths others are afraid to tread? Who will put down what they carry, their schedules, their lists? Who will put down their fears, their burdens? Who will present themselves to the King?

There is white all around her, a light I can see as well as touch. She walks through desert, city pavement, through detritus of war and gardens dripping from dew. She calls, her voice strong and loud in the night. She invites me to listen, to respond to the call of the faithful and brave.

I watch her. And I want to be her. I ache to rise with her, to say, "Yes, I am your sister, I see what you see, I am strong and bold and resolute, too." I want to join her and follow my King onto paths shadowed and dark, confident in his light, confident I am fierce, a light-bearer—I, too, a daughter of the King.

Shall we? Shall we join our sister and our King? Who will be healed and join in asking him to put salve on the places of pain— moments where evil ripped and violated? Who will come and be rescued? Who will come where they know there is help, and there is hope, and there is a place where each daughter can find shelter and be home?

Let us come. For we see her. And her. Sisters reaching their hands to touch the cloak of their Savior. Each a light bearer. Each alive and awake and walking. Each keeping the pace of her King.

FIND THE SHADOW UNDER THE WINGS, dear ones.

Follow the path that leads toward rescue and stay.

Wait and stay.

You will not be disappointed when Love finds you there.

You will not be looking this way or that for a different way to be filled.

No longer will anything else satisfy.

No longer will anything else quench your thirst.

Come, beauties, come and be fed and find shelter and be healed.

For I ask you to go forward, walking resolutely.

The beginning of the end and the beginning.

I will meet you there.

 **LISTEN**

Picture the woman described as Beauty walking. Sophie is drawn to her faith, her confidence in who she is and how she is loved. Beauty wants nothing to separate her from her God. Does Sophie want this too? What is your prayer to God in response?

THINK

> *Then the angel showed me the river of the water of life, bright as crystal,*
> *flowing from the throne of God and of the Lamb through the middle of*
> *the street of the city; also, on either side of the river, the tree of life with*
> *its twelve kinds of fruit, yielding its fruit each month. The leaves of the*
> *tree were for the healing of the nations. No longer will there be anything*
> *accursed, but the throne of God and of the Lamb will be in it,*
> *and his servants will worship him. They will see his face, and his name*
> *will be on their foreheads. And night will be no more. They will need*
> *no light of lamp or sun, for the Lord God will be their light,*
> *and they will reign forever and ever. (Revelation 22:1–5)*

1. How do you picture Sophie? What, to you, is beauty, strength, fearlessness, faith? In what specific way do you want to walk with Beauty and your King?

2. How do you imagine rising and walking with God, trusting him to lead you as you fight for the hearts of others who don't yet know him?

3. How is God uniquely asking you to follow him where you've never gone before?

TRUST

Go outside, or to a safe and quiet place, and lie down. Get comfortable. Close your eyes. Let your imagination show you Beauty walking. Watch her moving. Watch where she goes.

PRAY

Father, I want to be confident in you, walking with you in faith. Remove all doubt from me. Remind me that I am the daughter of a King, a King who became human and let himself be killed for a life I don't deserve. Let me live this life with integrity and courage and confidence, knowing my King, who conquered death, is before me; he has my hand; I will worship him forever. In your precious name, Jesus, Amen.

And Light Floods In

THERE IS A CIRCLE FORMING, and I can see it. You show me glimpses of it when I curl up next to you. Even in this noisy coffee shop where I write now, my fingers on these keys, a long line of people behind the chair where I sit, waiting to order. You show me glimpses of the circle, even when the world around me is full and busy and loud. Claire, who lifts her voice to you. Catherine, who ask for more faith. Johanna, who asks if you laugh. Hannah, who gives you her desire. Kate, who begs you to heal her. Jacqueline, who asks if you even care. Each of my friends, my sisters, you hold. Yes, in the circle. You are here too.

Father, we have trouble hearing you sometimes. We can't hear you when the space is full—too full—of false beliefs about you, about us. It's seems weird to me how the darkest whispers feel more familiar, more real than your voice, more safe, shadows over light.

We struggle to ask you to break a lie and show us truth. We struggle to hear you; lies we don't even know we believe are crowding you out.

Father, our prayers are questions, desperate scribbles in a journal at night: Do you love me? Can I love better? Do I even have any love to give? We want different answers than the ones we tell ourselves: Work harder to be a better mom. Work harder to be a better wife. Work harder to be a better Christian. Work harder to be a better person. Do you hear us, your daughters, shouting out the same prayers?

We struggle against you. Yet we are learning, helping one another know where to go when the lies come, when we believe we can't hear your voice in us. You gather us together. You gather us to you, into the circle where daughters come. You gather us and remind us, again, we are yours, we are loved, we are free.

Oh, God, we see your beauty here. And in your beauty we have eyes to see our beauty, the freedom that comes when we claim our place, when we bend our knees and let you take off the dark cloaks of shame that pressed us to the floor.

You are here, my God. You are here, in the circle, bending low. You are here, in the circle, where your daughters are held and rescued and found.

Help us hear you. Help us say *yes* to you. Help us let you in, no matter how difficult it feels. Help us be daughters who are known and fearless and grateful to pursue our identity, pursue community, and pursue adventure.

I GIVE YOU WORDS, MY LOVE. They are words from a place of love. Because you know you are loved and you are free, you are able to speak. Because you know you are adored and you are pursued, you are given voice to sing loud the cry of the claimed: You are chosen, you are delighted in, you are the one I wait here to see.

To all my daughters, listen close. I have something to say. In the moments when you feel fear overtake you, let me take your hand.

The circle has me at the center. Nothing else. It is a circle of hands clasped tight. Where daughters move in and out. But despite all movement, the circle remains.

Growing larger, yet staying intimate. It is a circle of understanding and freedom. It is a circle where joy is captured. It rises high.

I am the center of the circle, my daughters. I am the center of the joy, the creator of the joy and the beauty and the light.

And you were meant to dwell here. Forever.

 **LISTEN**

You, my sister, are part of this circle. Do you know that? What do you want to say about that? What is your prayer?

THINK

Now the Lord is the Spirit, and where the Spirit of the Lord is,
there is freedom. (2 Corinthians 3:17)

1. Sarabeth is in the circle. And you are there with her, one of the women, daughters of God. You are in the circle, living out your freedom, choosing to worship the King with your life. What keeps you from accepting this vision–seeing yourself in the circle, completely free, unencumbered, joy-filled, and radiant?

2. What gets in the way of you believing in beauty and hope and joy?

3. What does God say in response to Sarabeth that you want to hold close and remember?

 TRUST

Stand up. Lift up your hands. Open your fingers and pull your shoulders back so your arms are raised high. Make a joyful noise of celebration. Let your body move with the nudge of the Holy Spirit in you. You are in the circle, gathered up with God. You are filled with light.

 PRAY

Father, you come and rescue me. You invite me into a community, a family, a church where I am home. I open my hands and my heart. I receive your Spirit, and I am free. Help me stay close to you, walking with you, filled with your light and fresh air and new things. Amen.

Keep dreaming, my love.
Keep hoping, my love.
Keep listening for love songs,
for love is safe with me.

My Story

God's Words to Me

ACKNOWLEDGMENTS

Thank you to Judy Adams, who, over coffee at Cafe Baronne, was the first person to encourage me to craft these words into a book.

Thank you to the friends who cheered me on, read early versions, and encouraged me when I faced discouragement: Courtney Wagner, Jennifer Lundberg, Jinhee Kim, and Juliana Andersen. Your kindness was God's arm around me, saying, "Come on, girl. Keep going."

The biggest hug and gratitude to my LIFT sisters: Heather Fitzgerald, Heather Pietsch, Jen Durden, Kelly Morehead, Pyeatt Taylor, and Tina Rogers. You are the beauties who have stood by me, who have known and held my story, and who have shown me courage and faith in being vulnerable. I love you, friends.

Thank you to the sisters of Loop, the women who are right here with me, listening for God's whispers to their hearts. You encourage me, this beautiful community of God's girls. This book could not have been written without you.

My heartfelt thanks and gratitude to Don Jacobson, whose heart and vision and encouragement championed this project. Thank you for asking me, that one night, to read aloud with the voice God rescued and redeemed. I am so grateful.

Thank you to Paul Pastor, the most amazing wordsmith/prophetic editor I ever met, and the wise and brilliant Laurel Boruck and Tawny Johnson. The three of you, joining with Don and Martin Raz as the mighty Zeal Publishing team, pushed me even deeper to listening to the voices of the women in this book—stories that needed to speak. I am grateful I got to hear them and write them down.

My love and gratitude to my parents, Dennis and Pamela Johnson, cheerleading my writing for as long as I can remember.

Thank you to Justin, my husband and my dearest friend. You're the one who challenges me, loves me, and pushes me to listen to the Voice who knows me. Writing these words with you by my side . . . the best.

And my King, my Best Friend, my Savior, thank you. Thank you for these words, for your closeness, for your rescuing me and asking me to step forward, trust you more, desire your words more than anything else. It is your truth I want to hear and heed. Thank you for your whispers, for your voice in my heart, for the daughters here you adore. You are Love. Oh, how you love. Let us breathe you in.

INDEX

JENNIFER J. CAMP grew up in the middle of an almond orchard in Northern California. She was a small town girl who thought she wasn't good enough but who wanted everyone else to think that she was. The story she now loves to tell? It's the story of a lost girl and an almond tree and a gentle Savior who loves fierce. It's the story of a Savior who goes before us, wanting each of his daughters to know who she is, in Christ, and whose Voice she is made to sing.

The author of *Loop Devotional*—and a former high school English teacher—Jennifer loves to encourage people to seek and live out the truth of their story, their identity in Christ. Jennifer earned a teaching credential from UC Berkeley and a MA degree in English Education from Columbia University, Teacher's College, after graduating with a BA in English at UCLA. Jennifer and her husband, Justin Camp, are the cofounders of Gather Ministries (gatherministries.com), a nonprofit organization committed to bringing the genius of Jesus to the lives of busy women and men—women and men whose lives are filled but not full.

Jennifer spends her days trying to listen close to God's whispers, writing, and encouraging women to remember the truth of their identities, in Christ. She lives in the San Francisco Bay Area with Justin and their three awesome kids and would love to connect with you.

websites: jenniferjcamp.com, gatherministries.com, holyentanglement.com
Twitter: jenniferjcamp
Facebook: JenniferJCamp
Instagram: jenniferjcamp

ZEALbooks

Portland, Oregon

Zeal Books is a new publisher dedicated to world-changing ideas. We're focused and founded on love—love for our authors and love for their books. And love makes you zealous. Zeal's commitment to its authors, readers, and accounts is to only publish books we're zealous for—books the world needs.

Visit us online for news, resources, and more, at zealbooks.com, or find us on social media:

 @ZealBks

 @ZealBks

f facebook.com/zealbks